D1144419

Marigolds grow wild on platforms

An anthology of railway poetry

edited by
Peggy Poole

CASSELL

For Edward and Hannah – future travellers

Cassell Publishers Limited
Wellington House, 125 Strand, London WC2R 0BB

Introduction, selection and editorial matter copyright
© Peggy Poole 1996
Poems copyright authors and publishers (see Acknowledgements)

All rights reserved. No part of this publication may be reproduced or
transmitted in any form or by any means, electronic or mechanical,
including photocopying, recording or any information storage and
retrieval system, without permission in writing from the publishers.

First published 1996

British Library Cataloguing-in-Publication Data
A catalogue record for this book is available from the British Library

ISBN 0-304-34776-0

The editor and publishers are indebted to Robin Munro for the title of
this anthology, which comes from his poem 'The Galloway Line'

Designed by Gwyn Lewis

Cover illustration copyright © Jennie Tuffs 1996

Distributed in the United States by
Sterling Publishing Co. Inc.
387 Park Avenue South, New York, NY 10016–8810

Distributed in Australia by
Capricorn Link (Australia) Pty Ltd
2/13 Carrington Road, Castle Hill, NSW 2154

Typeset in Trump Medieval and Berkeley Old Style by
August Filmsetting, Haydock, St Helens
Printed and bound in Great Britain by Mackays of Chatham PLC,
Chatham, Kent

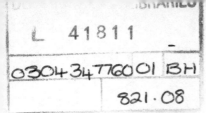
L 41811

0304 34776001 BH

821.08

CONTENTS

THREE   From a Railway Carriage

FOUR Oh, Mr Porter!

FIVE   The Permanent Way

SIX   Off the Rails

INTRODUCTION

Changing trains at Preston station a few years ago, on the way to give a reading at Windermere, I became aware that the station – all stations? – had a character, an atmosphere and an entity of its own, and that we, the travellers, were less important even than those proverbial ships in the night. Yet without us, their 'customers', no station would exist.

This started me thinking about railways, which resulted in hours spent, with official blessing, at Liverpool Lime Street – my local terminus – and led to a sequence of railway poems and a children's book. That, I thought, was the end. But how wrong I was. In February 1995 I suddenly became obsessed with the idea of an anthology of railway poems, and immediately they began to fly at me from every direction in bewildering numbers.

Why is it that trains and everything associated with them evoke such a massive response? Is it because our awareness is heightened when we travel, our antennae wave frantically, our emotions are hopelessly mixed, everything has a double or treble meaning? Many of us have traumatic memories involving railways: I waved goodbye to my elder brother at Canterbury East when he left to fight in Burma, never to return. I can still see the train disappearing into the distance.

There is, of course, time for reflection on a journey, reflection about the past and the future, about our place in the scheme of things. In fact, it seldom works like that – the scenery outside, the girl in the train and the passengers who 'sweat and snore', not to mention the delays and uncertain connections, all conspire against any attempt at reflection. E.M. Forster writes of stations being 'the gates to the Glorious and the Unknown'. Unknown certainly; glorious, I'm not so sure about.

Sir John Betjeman, a true railway fanatic, had a 'second dream'. In a BBC broadcast he revealed that he would have liked to have been a stationmaster in a small country station branch line (single track). Not all of us want that, least of all today, when such lines are being abandoned, but he does echo our affection for trains. Probably 99 per cent of us have travelled by train at some time in our lives, whether on holiday, to visit friends or to attend an important event or interview. Such journeys are woven into the fabric of our lives, and we do not forget them.

Brought together here are some of most people's favourite railway poems of the past, together with those that I think may become future favourites. Not all are of equal excellence, but each has a contribution to make. Poets often dismiss their earlier work, believing that their latest poem, which they 'scribbled on the way here', is better than anything they have previously written. They tend to forget that their assessment is coloured by the elation that comes from the very act of writing. Poems, like wine, mature with the years – think of Hardy, Wordsworth and Shakespeare.

In making this selection I have left out almost as much as I have included, and among those excluded is 'The Ballad of John Axon', which I heard Ewan McColl perform in the Royal Liverpool Philharmonic Hall some time in, I think, the 1960s. It was magic. But it does not come off the page with anything like the same emotive power as when it is spoken, and it is, in any case, very long. Hence my decision to omit it. I have also included only a sprinkling of poems from or about different countries. There is a wealth of material here, waiting to be brought together, but it would need, and merit, a separate volume.

It's been a joyful job putting the collection together, although the surgical selection has been painful, and there are several people I would like to thank: certain members of my family, whom I may have bored from time to time; friends and neighbours, who readily accepted the chaos in which I (ably abetted by a puppy) lived for many months while poetry magazines and collections and typescripts of railway poems took over the house; Anne Harvey, Alison Chisholm and Phoebe Hesketh for their advice and encouragement; Ann Warr for her diligence in proofreading; Barry Holmes for his expertise and enthusiasm; Gladys Mary Coles for her invaluable support; editors and fellow poets for their help with contacts and suggestions; and, of course, my local library.

Arthur Miller, in an interview in the *Independent* in April 1995, was quoted as saying: 'Generalization is the death of art. It's in the details where God resides. If I could pray for anything, it would be to get more details.' There are details enough in the following pages, I hope, to make this anthology something approaching a work of art.

Peggy Poole

ONE

The Black Statement of Pistons

LOCOMOTIVES AND TRAIN SETS

Engines in the National Railway Museum, York

So still they stand inside their tomb
it seems impossible that they
should once have torn the air apart
with thunderous wheels and whistle-screams,
and we forget the awesome power
they generated in their prime.

Paint bright as morning, spick and span,
polished like antique furniture,
their names as pure as trumpet notes:
Atlantic Coast Express, Mallard,
Green Arrow, Gladstone, Evening Star.
With them an era's dead and gone.

But let imagination ride,
and once again the night is split
with furnace flame and windows lit
and smoke like mist across the fields
and in and out of stooks and ricks
slip Red Dragon and Silver Fox.

In the last days of our lost ease,
through tall forests of mill chimneys,
Queen of Scots and Northumbrian
were on the inter-city run
and England seemed a stable place
when Master Cutler ran his race.

JOHN WARD *(b. 1915)*

The Rainhill Trials (October 1829)

The iron-clad monsters
Stood to attention
Spurting so much smoke
That even the most ferocious
Of dragons would have turned and run.

Crowds gathered at a safe distance.
They'd heard such tales of these creatures –
That cows dropped dead
In their speedy wake;
But worse much worse.

That they swallowed people whole
Through gaps in their sides
And swept them away
To far-off lands
Never to return.

Now here the baying beasts
Waited. Tamed and shackled
Straining to prove that they
Were the best and would
Have that place in history.

The *Cyclopede* ran well
At first, but faded fast.
While the *Novelty* sped
Quickly on, amazing watchers
Until its bellows burst.

The mighty *Sanspareil*
Charged on, until 'wounded'
It retired, weeping water
From a failed pump, then
Perseverance ran out of steam.

The ungainly *Rocket* stood proud
In victory, the judges satisfied,
Opposition defied. It moved forward
Knowing that we would
All follow on these 'right lines'.

SUE GERRARD *(b. 1954)*

On the Projected Kendal and Windermere Railway

Is then no nook of English ground secure
From rash assault? Schemes of retirement sown
In youth, and 'mid the busy world kept pure
As when their earliest flowers of hope were blown,
Must perish; – how can they this blight endure?
And must he too the ruthless change bemoan
Who scorns a false utilitarian lure
'Mid his paternal fields at random thrown?
Baffle the threat, bright Scene, from Orrest-head
Given to the pausing traveller's rapturous glance:
Plead for thy peace, thou beautiful romance
Of nature; and, if human hearts be dead,
Speak, passing winds; ye torrents, with your strong
And constant voice, protest against the wrong.

WILLIAM WORDSWORTH *(1770–1850)*

Liverpool Overhead Railway in the Thirties

Seventeen stations to Seaforth Sands,
their names a sort of History Quiz,
a mark for every one you knew:
Nelson, Clarence, Huskisson, Gladstone.
Journey's end, the *Caradoc* bar
and a congress of whores from Regent Road.
The Overhead drip-fed gutter-hungry
sailors, urgent to let the salt sea
out of their system for a night,
from ship to bar, from bar to bed,
and if their luck was in to ship again.
(If not, the lock-up, or a split head
and empty wallet down some dark ginnel.)

Six miles it stuttered and clattered over
bowstring bridges in which the gale sang.
To port, the river and half a hundred docks,
With piers, jetties, cranes, gantries,
and the lonely wail of sirens in sulphurous fog.
To starboard, empty warehouses,
as big as Pyramids; halftime mills;
mansions built from profit in slaves,
let out rooms to lascar greasers,
firemen from Lagos and Accra:
bed, chair, no oilcloth on the floor,
two bob a week. The fleas came free.

Meccano-construct of some mad engineer,
less magic carpet, more aerial tram,
it served as butt for adenoidal jokes
by those Murphys and Quinns who scuffed its boards
in hobnailed boots, settled ample backsides
on varnished slats, spat on its floor,
were hidden in acrid smokescreens
laid down by their gnarled and spittled clays,
and at the drop of a hat wore the Green

to burnish stories of old hungers, rapes,
massacres and half-forgotten wrongs.

Had its uses by darkness, too.
Under its watertight umbrella,
lost souls slept in sacks, dreamt of jobs,
of food, and fire, and fields of lavender.

JOHN WARD *(b. 1915)*

Steamboats, Viaducts, and Railways

Motions and Means, on land and sea at war
With old poetic feeling, not for this,
Shall ye, by Poets even, be judged amiss!
Nor shall your presence, howsoe'er it mar
The loveliness of Nature, prove a bar
To the Mind's gaining that prophetic sense
Of future change, that point of vision, whence
May be discovered what in soul ye are.
In spite of all that beauty may disown
In your harsh features, Nature doth embrace
Her lawful offspring in Man's art; and Time,
Pleased with your triumphs o'er his brother Space,
Accepts from your bold hands the proffered crown
Of hope, and smiles on you with cheer sublime.

WILLIAM WORDSWORTH *(1770–1850)*

The Express

After the first powerful plain manifesto
The black statement of pistons, without more fuss
But gliding like a queen, she leaves the station.
Without bowing and with restrained unconcern
She passes the houses which humbly crowd outside
The gasworks, and at last the heavy page
Of death, printed by gravestones in the cemetery.
Beyond the town, there lies the open country
Where, gathering speed, she acquires mystery,
The luminous self-possession of ships on ocean.
It is now she begins to sing – at first quite low
Then loud, and at last with a jazzy madness –
The song of her whistle screaming at curves,
Of deafening tunnels, brakes, innumerable bolts.
And always light, aerial underneath
Retreats the elate metre of her wheels.
Steaming through metal landscape on her lines,
She plunges new eras of white happiness
Where speed throws up strange shapes, broad curves
And parallels clean like trajectories from guns.
At last, further than Edinburgh or Rome,
Beyond the crest of the world, she reaches night
Where only a low stream-line brightness
Of phosphorus, on the tossing hills is white.
Ah, like a comet through flame, she moves entranced
Wrapt in her music no bird-song, no, nor bough,
Breaking with honey buds, shall ever equal.

STEPHEN SPENDER *(1909–95)*

Train Whistles
(For Sam)

The lagging wail of the hoarse-throated whistle
interrupts our sleep or work with equal impunity;
we cannot shut out, cannot resent
that relentless disposition to organize.
Watch out, move along, don't get caught.
We look up from our paper, book, cash-register
to note the time. 'Oh, yes, the eleven-thirty,'
as if seasons couldn't turn without that gear
running smoothly at the exact hour.
Or from a deep dream we rouse by degrees
to awareness of what the voice is,
not speaking names, but calling an event
as the string of empty coalcars travels south,
and we know the mines and miners wait stolidly.

Some elders recall whistles differently pitched
that told of passengers sliding quickly
through dozens of small-town stations.
To be a 'whistle-stop' was as much
as an insult to the grace
and sophistication of its residents,
for when they were especially lucky,
on events of monumental importance,
even they bought tickets and raced away
behind an imperious whistle.

That adventure loses reality, gains glamour
every year it recedes down the track;
our children ask incredulous questions
about how trains ran, that we answer
with smiles and metaphors and endless
testimony to the magic of a whistle

AMY JO SCHOONOVER (b. 1937)

To a Locomotive in Winter

THEE for my recitative,
Thee in the driving storm even as now, the snow, the winter-day
    declining,
Thee in thy panoply, thy measur'd dual throbbing and thy beat
    convulsive,
Thy black cylindric body, golden brass and silvery steel,
Thy ponderous side-bars, parallel and connecting rods, gyrating,
    shuttling at thy sides,
Thy matrical, now swelling pant and roar, now tapering in the
    distance,
Thy great protruding head-light fix'd in front
Thy long, pale, floating vapor-pennants, tinged with delicate
    purple,
The dense and murky clouds out-belching from thy smoke-stack,
Thy knitted frame, thy springs and valves, the tremulous
    twinkle of thy wheels,
Thy train of cars behind, obedient, merrily following,
Through gale or calm, now swift, now slack, yet steadily
    careering;
Type of the modern – emblem of motion and power – pulse of
    the continent,
For once come serve the Muse and merge in verse, even as here I
    see thee,
With storm and buffeting gusts of wind and falling snow,
By day thy warning ringing bell to sound its notes,
By night thy silent signal lamps to swing.

Fierce-throated beauty!
Roll through my chant with all thy lawless music, thy swinging
    lamps at night,
Thy madly-whistled laughter, echoing, rumbling like an
    earthquake, rousing all,

Law of thyself complete, thine own track firmly holding,
(No sweetness debonair of tearful harp or glib piano thine,)
Thy trills of shrieks by rocks and hills return'd,
Launch'd o'er the prairies wide, across the lakes,
To the free skies unpent and glad and strong.

WALT WHITMAN *(1819–92)*

585

I like to see it lap the Miles –
And lick the Valleys up –
And stop to feed itself at Tanks –
And then – prodigious step

Around a Pile of Mountains –
And supercilious peer
In Shanties – by the sides of Roads –
And then a Quarry pare

To fit its Ribs
And crawl between
Complaining all the while
In horrid – hooting stanza –
Then chase itself down hill –

And neigh like Boanerges –
Then – punctual as a Star
Stop – docile and omnipotent –
At its own stable door –

EMILY DICKINSON *(1830–86)*

The Train Spotter

Rather a timid child. Not good with girls
I chose the track-side of life but never cleared
my Thirty-Threes or saw a Western gallop
westward with the Cheltenham Spa Express –
a wildcat bobbing through the Wiltshire dust,
hydraulic paws punching loose fishplates.
I came too late or peaked or peaked too soon or something.

Once on a day-trip to York I did see
one of the last Deltics – I forget which –
but it roared like an oven and its wheels
squealed like a sack of kittens as it bit
its solid way south with a slow parcels.
As I tell the new lot, that was a real
sleepless-nights-of-wanting locomotive.

JONATHAN DAVIDSON *(b. 1964)*

Ghost Train

Ten o'clock at night on Stockport station:
My train's not due for a quarter of an hour.
The warm bright buffet-bar's still open, but
I've come outside for air. Closed silent trucks
Wall up the platform where I walk. Dirty
As scaffolding or used tarpaulin sheets
They are: just husks. The one clean thing on each
Is its nightly destination label –
Mouse-trap snapped; fresh-caught.
                    Behind and in the dark,
Shelled in by wood, by sacks, by envelopes,
Lie a whole day's thoughts of love and business
Waiting to bring tears or smiles or frowns.
The mail train jerks, and moves away. I hear
A thousand susurrations through its doors.

PETER WALTON *(b. 1936)*

Strange Call

The carriages move slowly,
drag and shunt their way
through maze of sidings, slide
into the corner of my vision,
away to their familiar reaches
unknown to me.

I stand above on a hilltop
watching early movement,
hearing faintly through the life roar far below
clank and throb of trains.

Some strange call
urges me backwards, forwards –
catapults me into regions –
where I can smile, regardless
that no one understands.

I move slowly, start to lumber
down the hill, and gather speed
racing, tumbling to tracks
until the hum and whistle
claim me, bind me to rails,
carry me away.

ALISON CHISHOLM *(b. 1952)*

Night Mail

I

This is the Night Mail crossing the Border,
Bringing the cheque and the postal order,

Letters for the rich, letters for the poor,
The shop at the corner, the girl next door.

Pulling up Beattock, a steady climb:
The gradient's against her, but she's on time.

Past cotton-grass and moorland border,
Shovelling white steam over her shoulder,

Snorting noisily, she passes
Silent miles of wind-bent grasses.

Birds turn their heads as she approaches,
Stare from bushes at her blank-faced coaches.

Sheep-dogs cannot turn her course;
They slumber on with paws across.

In the farm she passes no one wakes,
But a jug in a bedroom gently shakes.

II

Dawn freshens. Her climb is done.
Down towards Glasgow she descends,
Towards the steam tugs yelping down a glade of cranes,
Towards the fields of apparatus, the furnaces
Set on the dark plain like gigantic chessmen
All Scotland waits for her:
In dark glens, beside pale-green lochs,
Men long for news.

III

Letters of thanks, letters from banks,
Letters of joy from girl and boy,
Receipted bills and invitations
To inspect new stock or to visit relations,
And applications for situations,
And timid lovers' declarations,
And gossip, gossip from all the nations,
News circumstantial, news financial,
Letters with holiday snaps to enlarge in,
Letters with faces scrawled on the margin,
Letters from uncles, cousins and aunts,
Letters to Scotland from the South of France,
Letters of condolence to Highlands and Lowlands,
Written on paper of every hue,
The pink, the violet, the white and the blue,
The chatty, the catty, the boring, the adoring,
The cold and official and the heart's outpouring,
Clever, stupid, short and long,
The typed and the printed and the spelt all wrong.

IV

Thousands are still asleep,
Dreaming of terrifying monsters
Or a friendly tea beside the band in Cranston's or Crawford's;
Asleep in working Glasgow, asleep in well-set Edinburgh,
Asleep in granite Aberdeen,
They continue their dreams,
But shall wake soon and hope for letters,
And none will hear the postman's knock
Without a quickening of the heart.
For who can bear to feel himself forgotten?

W.H. AUDEN *(1907–73)*

25

Closely Observed Films

(The cinema's long romance with railways began in 1895,
when the first paying audience watched a 50-second sequence
of a train entering a French station. Many memorable arrivals
and departures have followed.)

Lights travel across a face from carriage windows;
Steam lingers, like a wound, in black and white;
Clipped voices ration feelings as in wartime,
An eyebrow lifts, a hand grazes a sleeve;
Outside a whistle shivers for departures.

We travel everywhere on single tickets,
Perfectly still, thrilled by perpetual motion;
Beginning to move through light's excited darkness
As out of stations, on shared, different journeys
Towards new destinations, sights and sounds

Like Asia, where a bamboo bridge explodes,
Or deserts as a Turkish engine keels
And ploughs a fatal furrow, or the camp
Where terror pens cowed women under wire,
We flinch beside them, yet on other days
We part a herd of bison, get up steam
To save a line and laugh at bureaucrats.

Drawn in by close-ups, swept by tracking shots,
We watch a child's toy cross a steppe's white winter;
Glimpse from a corridor a blazing car,
Set goggles for a survey from a footplate,
Chug out a summer's shunting in some sunshine

As light as Africa, where every halt
Has crowd scenes and a missionary with flowers,
Or India where a sage bows a farewell,
(We do not stay but leave him in his stillness).
Trains never wait; we have to let them go
Into slow fades and middle distances,

Whole century of memories since it started:
That fifty-second sequence, a French town,
A slow train edging to a flickering platform,
A simple journey on the edge of seats
Ending, like all the best, with no one moving.

MARTYN HALSALL (b. 1947)

Steam Day at Didcot

All along the line from Oxford station
bald men in macs behind their tripods stand,
while we all kings in our own estimation
steam triumphing through the breathless land.

By chance we're caught up in a national dream,
already fixed in a hundred genre photos,
all pilgrims puffing to a shrine of steam,
to Didcot with its resurrected locos.

The two old men beside us sit entranced.
They love the smoke that licks the window-glass
as once it always did. As we've advanced
so they've remained behind like nags at grass

framed in the fields the creaking train unreels.
And all along the coach the steam-buffs feed on
railway mags, their memories on rails
that lead back, rusting, to a steamy Eden.

And here at last is Didcot where the air
is sharp with coal, where pistons sheathed in grease
hiss mightily and stun small boys, and where
to stain the sky with smoke is no disgrace,

while in another steaming world quite near
gross cooling towers mouth clouds that one dislikes
because they foul the country atmosphere
and give fish acid-baths in Swedish lakes.

DAVID GILL (b. 1934)

27

Tank Engines Rule – O.K?

Though famous locomotives
Have thundered down the years,
There's only one small blue one
That chuffs in my son's ears.

The sidings are its milieu.
Can't pull a main line train.
It frustrates the Fat Controller
Treating shunting as a game.

Its stories make good reading.
It's often on tv
Although it may not go fast
It's a star, if you are three.

Rocket, Mallard, Scotsman,
Immortal steam-filled rank,
Their pulling power has nothing
To compete with Thomas the Tank.

HILARY TINSLEY *(b. 1949)*

My Train Set

I love to see my engine
Moving round the track.
I also like the lay-out
From my Hornby pack.

The signals and the signal box
Are standing by the rails;
The level crossing with the lights
Could stop the 'Prince of Wales'.

But when it gets used most of all
Is when my light is out.
Then I'm asleep, the house is quiet
Driver Dad's about.

TIMOTHY HEAL *(b. 1985)*

TWO

All Aboard

STATIONS, ARRIVALS AND DEPARTURES

Announcement

The 10.19 will call at Sideways Glance,
Eye Junction, Smile, and Unexpected Chance,
Then Disco, Party, Pub, and Country Walk,
And on to Intimacy, Bed and Talk,
Commitment, Mortgage, Offspring, Menopause,
Where it divides; passengers for Divorce
Should travel in the front. Any passenger
For Widowhood should travel in the rear.
A hot and cold service will be supplied
Throughout. We wish you all a pleasant ride.

ROD RIESCO *(b. 1949)*

Pershore Station, *or* A Liverish Journey First Class

The train at Pershore station was waiting that Sunday night
Gas light on the platform, in my carriage electric light,
Gas light on frosty evergreens, electric on Empire wood,
The Victorian world and the present in a moment's
    neighbourhood.
There was no one about but a conscript who was saying goodbye
    to his love
On the windy weedy platform with the sprinkled stars above
When sudden the waiting stillness shook with the ancient spells
Of an older world than all our worlds in the sound of the Pershore
    bells.
They were ringing them down for Evensong in the lighted abbey
    near,
Sounds which had poured through apple boughs for seven
    centuries here.
With Guilt, Remorse, Eternity the void within me fills
And I thought of her left behind me in the Herefordshire hills.
I remembered her defencelessness as I made my heart a stone
Till she wove her self-protection round and left me on my own.
And plunged in a deep self pity I dreamed of another wife
And lusted for freckled faces and lived a separate life.
One word would have made her love me, one word would have
    made her turn
But the word I never murmured and now I am left to burn.
Evesham, Oxford and London. The carriage is new and smart
I am cushioned and soft and heated with a deadweight in my
    heart.

JOHN BETJEMAN (1906–84)

Adlestrop

Yes. I remember Adlestrop –
The name, because one afternoon
Of heat the express-train drew up there
Unwontedly. It was late June.

The steam hissed. Someone cleared his throat.
No one left and no one came
On the bare platform. What I saw
Was Adlestrop – only the name.

And willows, willow-herbs and grass
And meadowsweet, and haycocks dry,
No whit less still and lonely fair
Than the high cloudlets in the sky.

And for that minute a blackbird sang
Close by, and round him, mistier,
Farther and farther, all the birds
Of Oxfordshire and Gloucestershire.

EDWARD THOMAS *(1878–1917)*

Not Adlestrop

Not Adlestrop, no – besides, the name
hardly matters. Nor did I languish in June heat.
Simply, I stood, too early, on the empty platform,
and the wrong train came in slowly, surprised, stopped.
Directly facing me, from a window,
a very, *very* pretty girl leaned out.

           When I, all instinct,
stared at her, she, all instinct, inclined her head away
as if she'd divined the much married life in me,
or as if she might spot, up platform,
some unlikely familiar.

For my part, under the clock, I continued
my scrutiny with unmitigated pleasure.
And she knew it, she certainly knew it, and would not
glance at me in the silence of not Adlestrop.

      Only when the train heaved noisily, only
when it jolted, when it slid away, only *then*,
daring and secure, she smiled back at my smile,
and I, daring and secure, waved back at her waving.
And so it was, all the way down the hurrying platform
as the train gathered atrocious speed
towards Oxfordshire or Gloucestershire.

DANNIE ABSE *(b. 1923)*

from Effingham Station

Effingham Station wooden fronted
Decants commuters tired and worn,
Harassed, haunted, gaunt and hunted
Crosswords finished, faces drawn.

Doting wives in waiting Datsuns
Manilow crooning on cassette
Peer through pouring rain at hats and
Coats and dearest getting wet.

★

Through Effingham Station early morning
Multiple units chatter and spark
The Southern Region station awning
Flashes bright blue in the dark.

Georgian postbox emptied daily
Stands like sentry on the green
Where life's tail-enders chat, and frailly
Clap the youths in cricket cream.

Effingham Common bright stream bordered
Flanked by cosy Surrey homes
Garden centre stocked, well ordered,
Bought with overdrafts and loans.

Open sports car neat two seater
Fifteen hundred MGA
Roars through Effingham like a cheetah
On into the cloudless day.

Thelwell tummied on the verges
Of the common cropping grass,
Jodhpured school girl coaxes, urges,
Clearly not gymkhana class.

★

Effingham Station wooden fronted
Decants commuters tired and worn,
Harassed, haunted, gaunt and hunted
Crosswords finished, faces drawn.

MIKE READ *(b. 1951)*

Suspense at Preston

Father said 'The viaducts are safe,
Founded on wool in shifting sand. That gash
Of quarry in the hill marks Carnforth, lass.
Look – boats abandoned up the banks of Lune –
We'll be in Preston soon . . .

''L'' stands for London (should be Lancashire)
In L.M.S.   Keep heads well in because
Of flying cinders. Telegraph wires
Make weaving patterns – modern artistry –
Soon have a cup of tea.'

Seen from the train nothing – yet all – was real;
A childhood tale created for a day,
The stations fable-lands, their people ghosts
Who haunted for an hour, then travelled on
In an endless search for home.

Marooned at Preston station, carriage-bound,
We'd wait, while (blithely, as if going to war)
Father thrust buffet-wards. Escaping steam
Hissed, and decamping wagons clanked through isles
Of grinding platform piles.

No one seemed anxious – only me.
I was in agony for his return.
He would become a shade, a transient thing
If left behind; and I an orphan, tossed
To chance, my brief world lost.

JEAN SERGEANT *(b.1928)*

Returning Home

I saw Virginia Woolf at Preston Station.
A woman with two hats on,
One a white sun hat, and above that
A wide-brimmed straw with a black band.
(Whom was she mourning?)
She'd lost a plastic bag
And flapped along the platform
Like a gull along the tide line,
Searching about the rows of metal seats,
She was tall and wore large shoes.
Her flowered skirt showed briefly
Below a belted summer mac.

Did she, I wondered, dream of waves
And a distant lighthouse,
Sun on a blind,
And the acorn blind-pull moving tentatively across the floor?

No one jeered at her.
One or two smiled wanly to themselves.
A well-fed station official,
Running down the platform with her bag,
Pursued her between concrete pillars.
Indifferent observers, waiting for other trains,
Were we the river stones in her pockets dragging her below the
    surface?

But then, I think she rose with slow wing-beats and moved away
Unrestrained
Over the swelling crests,
Into the spaces of her own mind.

JUDITH YOUNG *(b. 1928)*

Gare du Midi

A nondescript express in from the South,
Crowds round the ticket barrier, a face
To welcome which the mayor has not contrived
Bugles or braid: something about the mouth
Distracts the stray look with alarm and pity.
Snow is falling. Clutching a little case,
He walks out briskly to infect a city
Whose terrible future may have just arrived.

W.H. AUDEN *(1907–73)*

at the station

the snowflakes
white locusts
eat the sky
swirling to tears against warm lips
they bite at teeth and fingers
etch away the houses outlines
smother trees

here on the platform no one speaks
we stamp our feet like cattle
someone coughs

we wait for springtime
watching for the train.

RICHARD HILL *(b. 1941)*

In Freiburg Station

In Freiburg Station, waiting for a train,
I saw a Bishop in puce gloves go by.
Now God may thunder furious from the sky,
Shattering all my glory into pain,
And joy turn stinking rotten, hope be vain,
Night fall on little laughters, little loves
And better Bishops don more glorious gloves
While I go down in darkness; what care I?

There is one memory God can never break,
There is one splendour more than all the pain,
There is one secret that shall never die,
Star-crowned I stand and sing, for that hour's sake.
In Freiburg Station, waiting for a train,
I saw a Bishop with puce gloves go by.

RUPERT BROOKE *(1887–1915)*

Father in the Railway Buffet

What are you doing here, ghost, among these urns,
These film-wrapped sandwiches and help-yourself biscuits,
Upright and grand, with your stick, hat and gloves,
Your breath of eau-de-cologne?

What have you to say to these head-scarfed tea-ladies,
For whom your expensive vowels are exotic as Japan?
Stay, ghost, in your proper haunts, the clubland smokerooms,
Where you know the waiters by name.

You have no place among these damp and nameless.
Why do you walk here? *I came to say good-bye.*
You were ashamed of me for being different.
It didn't matter.

You who never even learned to queue?

U.A. FANTHORPE *(b. 1929)*

The Railway Tramp

Listening to the voices from within,
That he cannot lose no matter where he hide.
Likes the big city railway stations best,
Easy pickings and warm waiting rooms for rest.

No longer cares that people sometimes stare,
Some smile; most glad it isn't them standing there.

Draining the remaining dregs of binned pop cans,
Devouring left-over cheeseburger and chips,
Wiping grease onto the filthy suit bought when
A wife, kids and a car meant better times.

JOHN CRITCHLEY *(b. 1957)*

Down and Out, Paddington Station

Weighed down by paper bags
And tired string-tied coat
She shuffled among the tables
Inspecting the abandoned drinks
Then sat and dozed the timetable away
The faded hair told nothing
Above the lines of ingrained dirt
She had a little time
Before the midnight deadline
We did not know her destination –
Perhaps a doorway in the Euston Road
The cheerful flowers mocked her
Watched by unseeing
Sleeping the sleep of the unloved

CHRISTINE BOOTHROYD *(b.1934)*

In a Waiting-Room

On a morning sick as the day of doom
    With the drizzling gray
    Of an English May,
There were few in the railway waiting-room.
About its walls were framed and varnished
Pictures of liners, fly-blown, tarnished.
The table bore a Testament
For travellers' reading, if suchwise bent.

    I read it on and on,
And, thronging the Gospel of Saint John,
Were figures – additions, multiplications –
By some one scrawled, with sundry emendations;
    Not scoffingly designed,
    But with an absent mind, –
Plainly a bagman's counts of cost,
What he had profited, what lost;
And whilst I wondered if there could have been
    Any particle of a soul
    In that poor man at all,
    To cypher rates of wage
    Upon that printed page,
    There joined in the charmless scene
And stood over me and the scribbled book
    (To lend the hour's mean hue
    A smear of tragedy too)
A soldier and wife, with haggard look
Subdued to stone by strong endeavour;
    And then I heard
    From a casual word
They were parting as they believed for ever.

    But next there came
    Like the eastern flame
Of some high altar, children – a pair –
Who laughed at the fly-blown picture there.
'Here are the lovely ships that we,

Mother, are by and by going to see!
When we get there it's 'most sure to be fine,
And the band will play, and the sun will shine!'
It rained on the skylight with a din
As we waited and still no train came in;
But the words of the child in the squalid room
Had spread a glory through the gloom.

THOMAS HARDY *(1840–1928)*

At the Railway Station, Upway

'There is not much that I can do
For I've no money that's quite my own!'
Spoke up the pitying child –
A little boy with a violin
At the station before the train came in, –
'But I can play my fiddle to you,
And a nice one 'tis, and good in tone!'

The man in the handcuffs smiled;
The constable looked, and he smiled, too,
As the fiddle began to twang;
And the man in the handcuffs suddenly sang
With grimful glee:
'This life so free
Is the thing for me!'
And the constable smiled, and said no word,
As if unconscious of what he heard;
And so they went on till the train came in –
The convict, and boy with the violin.

THOMAS HARDY *(1840–1928)*

Station Buffet

Put fifty pence more in the juke-box
as the music flows round and around
and we'll try to pretend I'm not leaving
I can cry without making a sound

as the singer sighs out all his troubles
in the soft notes I'm going to drown
for I'm going to prove I can lose in one move
my love and my town,
my love and my town

as we look at the rings made by coffee
and I look at my finger still bare
in moments my train will be leaving
my home and I'm leaving you there

and I wait for the music to take me
the only direction is down
for I'm going to prove I can lose in one move
my love and my town,
my love and my town

the hopscotch we played round the abbey
the kisses we shared in the park
memories cut like a knife as they turn off the lights
and I'm left all alone in the dark

the song ends and leaves me in silence
and I force back my tears with a frown
for I'm going to prove I can lose in one move
my love and my town
my love and my town.

PATRICIA FRAZER *(b. 1959)*

Waiting to be Met

(An Evacuee, 1940)

A child, too big to cry
I'd grown up in that year of war,
'was old enough' they said
to travel far; loneliness, a familiar friend,
came with me. The guard had helped me
to descend, unloading bag with me, clutching
my gas-mask in its cardboard box, the pocket game.
He'd asked, in his country drawl
'You know her name?'
He meant the woman coming to collect me.
No one came.

The silence was immense
after the train had gone;
late sunlight daubed the wooden seat,
the picket fence, against which I leant
too big to cry, and waited.
No one came.

I thought I heard a clock chime five
tolling into emptiness and fear;
then footsteps hurrying near, and through the gate
the woman came, unsmiling,
to take me to her home.
I stayed two years, but even now,
it seems upon reflection, that
no one ever came at Trowbridge Station.

DORIS CORTI (b. 1928)

The Metropolitan Railway. Baker Street Station Buffet

Early Electric! With what radiant hope
   Men formed this many-branched electrolier,
Twisted the flex around the iron rope
   And let the dazzling vacuum globes hang clear,
And then with hearts the rich contrivance fill'd
Of copper, beaten by the Bromsgrove Guild.

Early Electric! Sit you down and see
   'Mid this fine woodwork and a smell of dinner,
A stained-glass windmill and a pot of tea,
   And sepia views of leafy lanes in PINNER –
Then visualize, far down the shining lines,
Your parents' homestead set in murmuring pines.

Smoothly from HARROW, passing PRESTON ROAD,
   They saw the last green fields and misty sky,
At NEASDEN watched a workmen's train unload,
   And, with the morning villas sliding by,
They felt so sure on their electric trip
That Youth and Progress were in partnership.

And all that day in murky London Wall
   The thought of RUISLIP kept him warm inside;
At Farringdon that lunch hour at a stall
   He bought a dozen plants of London Pride;
While she, in arc-lit Oxford Street adrift,
Soared through the sales by safe hydraulic lift.

Early Electric! Maybe even here
   They met that evening at six-fifteen
Beneath the hearts of this electrolier
   And caught the first non-stop to WILLESDEN GREEN,
Then out and on, through rural RAYNER'S LANE
To autumn-scented Middlesex again.

Cancer has killed him. Heart is killing her.
   The trees are down. An Odeon flashes fire
Where stood their villa by the murmuring fir
   When 'they would for their children's good conspire.'
Of their loves and hopes on hurrying feet
Thou art the worn memorial, Baker Street.

                    JOHN BETJEMAN *(1906–84)*

The Wayside Station

Here at the wayside station, as many a morning,
I watch the smoke torn from the fumy engine
Crawling across the field in serpent sorrow.
Flat in the east, held down by stolid clouds,
The struggling day is born and shines already
On its warm hearth far off. Yet something here
Glimmers along the ground to show the seagulls
White on the furrows' black unturning waves.

But now the light has broadened.
I watch the farmstead on the little hill,
That seems to mutter: 'Here is day again'
Unwillingly. Now the sad cattle wake
In every byre and stall,
The ploughboy stirs in the loft, the farmer groans
And feels the day like a familiar ache
Deep in his body, though the house is dark.
The lovers part
Now in the bedroom where the pillows gleam
Great and mysterious as the deep hills of snow,
An inaccessible land. The wood stands waiting
While the bright snare slips coil by coil around it,
Dark silver on every branch. The lonely stream
That rode through darkness leaps the gap of light,
Its voice grown loud, and starts its winding journey
Through the day and time and war and history.

                    EDWIN MUIR *(1887–1959)*

Jubilate – Railway Imperial

I

They are forever fixed in time,
Closeted waxwork time,
In Eighteen Ninety Seven.

Within the ante-room the Munchi sits
Sashed, turbaned, beside a teapot
And expectant, upturned cups.

The Royal Waiting Room is snug.
Fire crimsons the grate.
Imagination crackles coals.

White-gloved, the balding Prince of Wales
Leans on the mantelpiece,
Tight in his braided jacket.

Next to him, elegant on the settee,
Alexandra is arranged – parasoled,
Ribboned, feathered and furbelowed.

Dominant in this room: Victoria –
Queen and Empress, black and silver caped,
Solemn with sixty Jubilee years.

Outside, the Royal Train, 'The Queen',
Waits to set down her principal guests
On to a platform pristine-clean.

The engine, heavy with Royal coats of arms,
Bears its own burnished majesty
And heads six opulent coaches.

Burnished and braided, David Hughes,
The train-driver, consults his watch.
His timekeeping challenges Big Ben's.

Some minutes forward in time,
Under the glass cage of the station-roof,
Another tableau – joyful with bunting.

The Coldstream Guards present arms.
One dips the colour in salute.
Waiting carriages stand to attention.

Two Empresses, two Victorias,
Take precedence. Lord Salisbury,
Prime Minister, shows deference.

Blue and white sailor-suited
Maurice, youngest Royal grandchild,
Clings to his mother's hand.

II

In real time, in actuality,
Did prescient thoughts cloud this celebration?
Did Queen Victoria herself foresee
The black-draped gathering within this station
Less than four years ahead? This time the Royal Train
Would be her catafalque, each metal plate,
Each timbered strut, immaculate, the pain
Of world-wide sorrow at her death innate;
One final plume of smoke from banked-down coals
Its own salute on her last railway journey,
David Hughes once more her driver. As shoals
Of tourists come in present time to see
The waxwork Jubilee presentations, do they
Reflect upon the transience of steam,
Of life, as they record their family day
By camera, camcorder, flashlight beam?
                    My grandfather,
                    Both Coldstream Guard
                    And railway timekeeper,
                    Wept when Victoria died.

BERYL CROSS *(b. 1929)*

Remembering Peter

I remember him at stations, poppy cheeks
A short walk from the steam
Suitcases puffing his wide girth
And an English laugh.

So few summers we brought him north
To the stag-sharp moors, days cut from quartz
The amethyst hills with their bloom of curlew
They filled his veins and ran his eyes.

I remember when he failed, his heart's drum dead
Only a thin loam lingered by his winter tomb
Rain hissing in the leaves and silver-belled
The station was unmanned for me
The train long broken down.

Now I am older, made of rusted losses
Grown used to grave years, staunch of grieving
Still he comes down the platform of my childhood days
With all the other things I lost to ghosts.

KENNETH STEVEN *(b. 1968)*

Holidays: Platform 8

They wait.
Dad's over-timed with work.
Mum's anxious, worried.
And the deep pit of the track is black.
Come back! she calls to the small child.
Baby screams.

The money's scarce. Her husband sighs.
He thinks of miracles – walking on seas.
Remember Icarus who flew too near the sun:
Enthusiasm kills see.
No heat. No sweat. Stay cool.
Rule is 'Live within your means.'

The children sing:

Clap! Dance! Clap! Dance!
Clap! Dance! Clap! Dance!
Boys have muscles.
Teacher can't count.

The north.
Wet slate. Damp leaves.
Factories with broken windows.
Rubble. Dirt. Puddle. Skip.

Clap! Dance! Clap! Dance!

PENZANCE! – coming in.

WENDY BARDSLEY *(b. 1944)*

Arrival in Nottingham

The train
trundles
over the Beeston Canal
with swans cruising up past barges parked townward
into that long
track-covered curve
of ground
Stops
in the Goods Yard North
for passengers
to take stock
of the view
of the castle
standing at
the other end
of the curve's radius,
impressive,
imposing
on its solid rock foundation
Shunts forward
into the Goods Yard West
Further aspects
of the castle
Lurches gradually
into the Goods Yard East
leaving the castle
behind an engine shed
Reaches
eventually
the station.

GERALD ENGLAND *(b. 1946)*

Making Connections

Passengers talk through a porthole
to a man in a glass tank.
He has red-rimmed eyes
and a rubber stamp.

A scant metal bridge, humped
like the one on the Willow Pattern plate, spans
two platforms and a view
of the lost igloo city of cars
painted by children.

There's a photograph booth
(against loss of identity en route),
a news stand with 'The Plain Truth'
available free, in a dark corner,
and a row of telephone cotes
to home in the lonely.

I eavesdrop the news –
'He should be here at twelve minutes past four'
(Twelve minutes past, repeated,
as if repetition will bring him for sure) –
and wait for her

who is too young to be running over bridges
after love and trains –
this little go-between, this bridge-hopper
moonlighting between mother and father.

Small as the Chinaman on the plate
she waddles across the bridge with her case.
'Why didn't you telephone me yesterday?' I scold
waving love's big stick.

DIANA HENDRY *(b. 1941)*

Amtrak Return

We stepped down from the high-riding train
as from the clouds
to where, on the platform,
our small family of three stood waiting,
bright welcome in their eyes
and in their hugs
though we had parted from them
for only four days.

Home-coming is to people
as well as to place.

MARY HODGSON *(b. 1927)*

Meeting the Empty Train

I wait and watch as winter scythes the air,
surprised its blast cannot disperse the stench
of oil, or swirl dust mounds beyond the bench
to reach the litter piles below the stair.
Twilight comes quickly now, and everywhere
the grimy lamps are being lit to drench
each platform. Faces pale as lovers wrench
themselves apart with sighs of taut despair.

I wrap my coat more tightly. I can feel
the empty places deep inside of me
that once you occupied, fight to conceal
the secret loss I want no one to see.
I count the trains that come, the trains that go,
as furrowed tracks drag me from all I know.

ALISON CHISHOLM *(b. 1952)*

Departures

Set in a floral arcade,
These are the dreams of departures, in which
The ancient climbing roses are always
In bloom beneath the shivering glass
Of the station's forcing-house. Although
Figures must dwindle and twined fingers
Have to unclasp, the backward look
Stays for ever. On cheeks high-toned
With grief, a single frozen tear.

But dreams are dreams – already
The first bend has removed the station
From view, and the shapely words of thanks
And farewell no longer make sense as the engine
Rattles through landscapes to which they belong
Not at all. Accept, nonetheless,
This real ghost train of gratitude, of words
Marshalled before, to be printed after,
As the lights of the carriages shrink into darkness.

LAWRENCE SAIL *(b. 1942)*

The Leave Train

The train is moving;
Out of the window I'm waving;
Sister, daughter, friend, and son
Wait on the platform unaware
The train has gone.

Behind them, relations, people
At parties, in shops, in the street –
People I know by sight but not to meet:
They cannot see
The light gone green for me
On a line untravelled.
One day they, one at a time,
Will take the train,
Each to a different destination
Not yet printed in the guide.
Yet every ticket's ordered in advance.

Under the clock they hurry
Home and back again
Making a dance of the time-table, believing
The train they must catch
Is not yet running.

PHOEBE HESKETH *(b. 1909)*

Railroad Station

All life is little railroad stations,
he murmured as he bent over her
like the older Gary Cooper, to say
goodbye; though he wore no hat,
no soft hat. Then he hitched up his
dun-coloured Brooks Brothers suit
over his furry stomach – how
she would miss nosing her way up
or down his furry stomach. Sure,
she answered under the low cirrus
dun-coloured in the orange lights
of the platform, all's arrival and de-
parture; looking just as wan as a
girl in a film still set in Minnesota.
Still, she blew a kiss or more
as the train ranted out, on its way
to connections she with her single
'55 Studebaker did not aspire to
(he was the worldly guy); and felt
her thin hair drawn back
in the starlight into a pony-tail.

Departures are worse, she thought
suddenly, acidly, in the station-
master's torch's gleam and regretted
he'd gone, she'd like to have called
that last thing, just on the hoot
of the train and seen, as he'd bent
to light up his pipe in the carriage,
his eyelids flicker in the glow.

JUDITH KAZANTZIS

Holiday's End

from 'Scenes from a Suburban Childhood'

In the corner seat of the compartment,
The buttoned moquette prickly to short-trousered legs,
I waited for the train's departure.
I could see the sun-patterned platform
Through the lowered leather-stropped window,
And sense the warm air gentle with smoke and engine oil,
As I listened to kindly Mrs McKenzie saying goodbye,
Her braided hair held in place
By a coiled tortoiseshell ear trumpet.
Too soon the train eased its way out of the station
To a light concerto of steam, wheels and rails,
And the platform moved away.
A last wave and the smarting salt came.
Tears for the end of a holiday?
Farewell Mrs McKenzie? Farewell sea?
Or for an awareness
Which I still carry with me?

JOHN COTTON *(b. 1925)*

On the Departure Platform

We kissed at the barrier; and passing through
She left me, and moment by moment got
Smaller and smaller, until to my view
    She was but a spot;

A wee white spot of muslin fluff
That down the diminishing platform bore
Through hustling crowds of gentle and rough
    To the carriage door.

Under the lamplight's fitful glowers,
Behind dark groups from far and near,
Whose interests were apart from ours,
    She would disappear,

Then show again, till I ceased to see
That flexible form, that nebulous white;
And she who was more than my life to me
    Had vanished quite . . .

We have penned new plans since that fair fond day,
And in season she will appear again –
Perhaps in the same soft white array –
    But never as then!

– 'And why, young man, must eternally fly
A joy you'll repeat, if you love her well?'
' – O friend, nought happens twice thus; why,
    I cannot tell!'

THOMAS HARDY *(1840–1928)*

After a Departure

Intimate god of stations,
on long, faded afternoons
before impatient trains depart,
when the aching lovers wait
and mothers embarrass sons,
discover your natural art;
delicately articulate
an elegy of the heart
for horizons appropriate,
or dialogues for the stage
and the opening of an eye.

Love invents the sadness of
tolerable departures.
So bless every fumbling kiss
when eyes, hands, lips, betray
shy, tentative disclosures,
conclusions that non-lovers miss.
Taxis, buses, surge away
through the grey metropolis
while mortals frown for words to say,
and their ordinary messages
approximate, therefore lie.

Those heroes who departed
spouting famous monologues
were more verbose than we.
Antony at Paddington,
bizarre in his Roman togs,
a sword clanking on his knee,
would have jabbered on and on
love epithets most happily,
well after the train had gone.
Let prosy travellers rage
long as Cleopatras sigh.

Romeo's peroration
for Juliet at Waterloo,
as gulps of steam arise
from the engine on its bit,
and from station-masters too,
would bring tears to the eyes.
Sooty god of stations permit
your express to dally, revise
timetables, dull schedules if it
allows one more classic page
or a Juliet to cry.

Today, I, your professional
pleb of words who must appear
spontaneous, who knows form
to be decorative logic,
whose style is in the error,
ask forgiveness for my storm
of silence when all speech grew sick;
who, waving from the platform,
found even gesture ironic,
afraid of your beautiful coinage
'I love you' and 'Goodbye'.

DANNIE ABSE *(b. 1923)*

The Home Front

from 'Points of Departure'

She measured their life by the station clock's moon-face
Which hoisted a spear-head from minute to minute
With juddering thumps like the guns in his letters
Or setting a pace for the leap of her panic
Until he stepped off in a milkyway steamburst
And into her arms for the precious duration.

Then where they embraced was their own constellation
Of whistles and flags and irrelevant trolleys
Dissolving too soon to the damp hiss of pistons
Beneath that same clock-face's minute to minute
Remorseless invasion, its blank valedictory
Bayonet charge on the ground of their parting.

JOHN MOLE *(b.1941)*

A Parting-Scene

The two pale women cried,
　But the man seemed to suffer more,
　　Which he strove hard to hide.
They stayed in the waiting-room, behind the door,
Till startled by the entering engine-roar.
As if they could not bear to have unfurled
Their misery to the eyes of all the world.

　A soldier and his young wife
　Were the couple; his mother the third,
　　Who had seen the seams of life.
He was sailing for the East I later heard.
– They kissed long, but they did not speak a word;
Then, strained, he went. To the elder the wife in tears
　'Too long; too long!' burst out. ('Twas for five years.)

THOMAS HARDY *(1840–1928)*

The Send-off

Down the close, darkening lanes they sang their way
To the siding-shed,
And lined the train with faces grimly gay.

Their breasts were stuck all white with wreath and spray
As men's are, dead.

Dull porters watched them and a casual tramp
Stood staring hard,
Sorry to miss them from the upland camp.
Then, unmoved, signals nodded, and a lamp
Winked to the guard.

So secretly, like wrongs hushed-up, they went.
They were not ours:
We never heard to which front these were sent.

Nor there if they yet mock what women meant
Who gave them flowers.

Shall they return to beatings of great bells
In wild train-loads?
A few, a few, too few for drums and yells,
May creep back, silent, to still village wells
Up half-known roads.

WILFRED OWEN *(1893–1918)*

The End of a Leave

Out of the damp black light,
The noise of locomotives,
A thousand whispering,
Sharp-nailed, sinewed, slight,
I meet that alien thing
Your hand, with all its motives.

Far from the roof of night
And iron these encounter;
In the gigantic hall
As the severing light
Menaces, human, small,
These hands exchange their counters.

Suddenly our relation
Is terrifyingly simple
Against our wretched times.
Like a hand which mimes
Love in this anguished station
Against a whole world's pull.

ROY FULLER *(1912–91)*

King's Cross to Liverpool

Clinging to small essentials, cup and comb
We have entrained, half-knowing what we did;
Now we have slept our last long night at home,
Stuck 'CABIN' on our lives and closed the lid.
How many months before we savour rightly
This gentle land that now we leave so lightly?

LISBETH DAVID *(b. 1923)*

Waving Goodbye

Laugh and the skin holds tighter. One word
and it's enough sometimes
to barrel a hole through the head.
Light spills aimlessly into the many rooms
where we might have met, said
what we might have said,
illuminates passing trains with an underground glare.
Now the face won't
come quite
into focus despite the turning, the turning.
Trains move in and out of stations.
Hands shake. Sometimes
one blurred eye is landscape
or you stand at the unreal point where lines converge.
They all advance behind their shrinking smiles
to greet a greeting. But then
there is this platform
where someone vanishes with tightly folded arms.
The train recedes on complicated rails.
Sit here quietly with a gutted skull, waving.

SYLVIA KANTARIS *(b. 1936)*

Communication Cord

A train draws out
With a fringe of waving hands
Circling in air, reluctantly unwinding
A thread of stretching air;
And those on the platform walk
After the train and wave, as if they could
Pull back the train with scarves;
Then at the bend
The hands are taken from sight
And the platform people
Suddenly drop their waving and turn away.
The cord is broken
And lies withered as wire, an empty railway line
Beside which we endure
Each from the clumsy surgery of goodbye
A haemorrhage of love.

FRANCES HARLAND

Parting in Wartime

How long ago Hector took off his plume,
Not wanting that his little son should cry,
Then kissed his sad Andromache goodbye –
And now we three in Euston waiting-room.

FRANCES CORNFORD (1886–1960)

from On Embarkation

In all the ways of going who can tell
The real from the unjustified farewell?
Women have sobbed when children left for school
Or husbands took the boat train to pursue
Contracts more tenuous than the marriage vow.
But now each railway station makes and breaks
The certain hold and drifts us all apart.
Some women know exactly what's implied.
Ten Years, they say behind their smiling eyes,
Thinking of children, pensions, looks that fade,
The slow forgetfulness that strips the mind
Of its apparel and wears down the thread;
Or maybe when he laughs and bends to make
Her laugh with him she sees that he must die
Because his eyes declare it plain as day.
And it is here, if anywhere, that words
– Debased like money by the same diseases –
Cast off the habitual clichés of fatigue
– The women hoping it will soon blow over,
The fat men saying it depends on Russia –
And all are poets when they say Goodbye
And what they say will live and fructify.

ALUN LEWIS *(1915–44)*

No Day Returns

From this place of parting and departure
see curvature of steel slice out of sight,
singing of static speed, in frozen flight.
Scimitar shapes, dissecting distances,
permanent way to sever local love,
permanent way, transient travellers
timetabled traffic burrowing bridges
carving through cuttings, slamming through stations
along embankments where wild flowers wave.
Transporting me again in space and time
recalling holidays of other days
bucket and spaded journeys to the sea
sunshine on sand and orgies of ice cream,
arrivals and departures, in brown, barometered hallways
of sundry Sunnyhaven or Seaview.
Later journeys, visits to far places
recall obscure, the reasons obsolete
I reset all the pivot points of change
but arrive only at the here and now.
Now, I will wait no more beneath the clock,
reunion half hoped for overdue
presume permanent parting of the way,
on this journey it seems, no day returns.

MIKE RATHBONE *(b. 1944)*

THREE

From a Railway Carriage

LOOKING OUT, LOOKING IN

Midnight on the Great Western

In the third-class seat sat the journeying boy,
   And the roof-lamp's oily flame
Played down on his listless form and face,
Bewrapt past knowing to what he was going,
   Or whence he came.

In the band of his hat the journeying boy
   Had a ticket stuck; and a string
Around his neck bore the key of his box,
That twinkled gleams of the lamp's sad beams
   Like a living thing.

What past can be yours, O journeying boy
   Towards a world unknown,
Who calmly, as if incurious quite
On all at stake, can undertake
   This plunge alone?

Knows your soul a sphere, O journeying boy
   Our rude realms far above,
Whence with spacious vision you mark and mete
This region of sin that you find you in,
   But are not of?

THOMAS HARDY *(1840–1928)*

One Way Journey

Preparations for leaving
went smoothly; cases were packed
last farewells made, friends
at the same stage gathered
to wish each other luck.
Untried adult stances were adopted
childish things put away
in biblical style.

We travelled south
by train together
controlled and positive –
the last extension of the thread.
Suddenly you held out
your ticket as if it was
obscene, and panic-stricken said
'A *single* ticket!'

My reply was designed
to reassure but my heart
could only tremble as you
glimpsed reality.

Now years later you speak
from distant lands, accomplished
in new skills; yet at times
that desperate note still sounds
'A *single* ticket!'

Beloved daughter, even love
cannot issue a return.

PEGGY POOLE *(b. 1925)*

from Old Woman on a Train

I wonder where you're going
Old woman on a train?
The hour so early
That you're wisely munching
Breakfast from plastic bag
That's lying
Upon your shrunken lap.

You do not seem to
Mind that I'm watching you
From opposite seat;
Noting the absorption,
Total, with which you eat
Crispbread and
Banana, bar of dried fruit.

Eyes rheumy, filming
Blueness half-drowned now
Red-rim-encircled,
Yet still darting lively
Intelligent glances
That shrewdly
Assess what's around you.

Next comes the terminus
Old woman on a train.
I watch you packing
Food papers back in your bag;
Carefully drawing-on
Brown mittens
That sheathe your gentle claws.

Where are you going
Old woman on a train?
I linger to note that
Your footstep's still sprightly;

See you drawn into the
Body-abrading
Shingle that's sucked underground.

You've set me wondering
Old woman on a train:
Will old age find me
Like you, time-eroded
To inner-smoothness, and kindly?
Old woman,
If so, I'll not complain.

MOLLIE MOORHILL *(1920–89)*

Railway Song

We're gliding through the countryside at ninety miles an hour,
Past dapple woods and meadows – orchards white with flower.
With here some speckled sunshine and there a shower of rain,
Haa-ow shriek the bridges at the passing of the train.

In gardens of the little town there's washing flying high,
A wind that we can't feel at all will surely blow it dry.
A silent brass band in the park will play to us in vain,
For all we hear is diddley-dum and the rattle of the train.

There are little country stations which the train goes rushing
    through
And crossings when the driver blows a warning blast or two.
De-dar, the points re-echo and repeat themselves again,
Oh the rhythm's half the magic of a journey in the train.

There are children playing in the fields, with a kite up in the sky
Who'll be lost to us for ever once the train's gone gliding by.
So watch the landscape closely for you'll never see again
What's streaming past the window as we travel in the train.

MARGARET CURWEN

The Guard's Van

The classless accommodation –
But I am merely mail, post.
I am sure of one thing:
Although I resemble
A tatty old dummy
As I sit slumped in my
Wheelchair – fake fur coat, a dated hat
Why a deerstalker? –
Is this any reason to be set aside
Banned from enjoying the company of society
Who are train travellers,
Presumably my so-called peers?
Oh no. How many times
Must I convince myself
The answer is in the negative?
Meshing, cage, bars around me
Why in this day and age must I bear
To be treated like a zoological exhibit?
I do not bite, I am not savage.
I dream about luxurious seats,
Tables and conversation;
Smells that make my stomach rumble,
The washing machine's turn.
The guards, my prison officers (warders)
Hardly have time even to spare a minute to converse with me
During my transportation.

So I wish to protest:
For my feeling is
That articles sent through the Royal Mail system
Receive far more care,
As if they are –

Yes, as if they are –
Newly born babies,
Than the disabled population enjoy.
I steam with anger.

Call me the Headline Express.

JOHNATHAN WOOD (b. 1968)

In a Railway Compartment

OXFORD to London, 1884:
Against the crimson arm-rest leant a girl
Of ten, holding a muff, twisting a curl,
Drumming her heels in boredom on the floor
Until a white-haired gentleman, who saw
She hated travelling, produced a case
Of puzzles: 'Seven Germans run a race . . .
Unwind this maze, escape the lion's paw . . .
The princess must be lowered by her hair . . .'
The train entered a tunnel, shrieking, all
The lights went out and when he took her hand
She was the princess in the tower and
A lion faced her on the moonlit wall
Who roared and reached and caught and held her there.

JOHN FULLER (b. 1937)

Breakfast Call

A Pullman breakfast
probably makes the most
perfect start to a day.
Sliding down the west coast
on buttery kippers, tea,
marmalade and toast.

But something insidious
has invaded the bliss
of early morning diners.
There's an annoying hiss
from stereo headphones;
but, even worse than this,

in striped shirts and braces,
middle management clones
swarm to corporate hives
with other city drones
and insist on prattling
loudly on poser phones.

Everyone must be told
they're travelling on a train.
So no one sleeps as blop,
blip, bleeps inflict the brain
and each short tunnel makes
blip bleeping start again.

Phones put down on tables
are itches which won't wait
to be scratched and take pride
of place among the plates.
They throb, egging on their
johns to communicate.

Surely they can't expect
others to be impressed;
not when forced to listen
to the career obsessed,
making trivial calls,
before common folk are dressed.

MALCOLM TAYLOR *(b. 1948)*

Like the Train's Beat

Like the train's beat
Swift language flutters the lips
Of the Polish airgirl in the corner seat.
The swinging and narrowing sun
Lights her eyelashes, shapes
Her sharp vivacity of bone.
Hair, wild and controlled, runs back:
And gestures like these English oaks
Flash past the windows of her foreign talk.

The train runs on through wilderness
Of cities. Still the hammered miles
Diversify behind her face.
And all humanity of interest
Before her angled beauty falls,
As whorling notes are pressed
In a bird's throat, issuing meaningless
Through written skies; a voice
Watering a stony place.

PHILIP LARKIN *(1922–85)*

from Strugnell's Sonnets

Indeed, 'tis true. I travel here and there
On British Rail a lot. I've often said
That if you haven't got the first-class fare
You really need a book of verse instead.
Then, should you find that all the seats are taken,
Brandish your Edward Thomas, Yeats or Pound.
Your fellow-passengers, severely shaken,
Will almost all be loath to stick around.

Recent research in railway sociology
Shows it's best to read the stuff aloud:
A few choice bits from Motion's new anthology
And you'll be lonelier than any cloud.
This stratagem's a godsend to recluses
And demonstrates that poetry has its uses.

WENDY COPE *(b. 1945)*

The Placid Gentleman

You know, said the placid gentleman on my right,
calmly wiping his glasses: you know, it's true;
we fear the Reds, and dentists, and cancer and tax,
until we forget there is anything else to do.

Believe me, he added, earnestly holding me
with a smeary bifocal gaze: if we could forget
our fear, and luxuriate in the good we have,
the result would be our finest hour yet.

I smiled and nodded. After all, how can you snort
or disagree in a crowded train? How say:
I am young, clear-eyed, tomorrow is what I would have,
and my paper warns it may well be blasted away?

P. ALAMIE PAGE

Strangers on a Train

We are customers on each side
of an Intercity table
you in your corner, I in mine.
We don't talk nor do you
catch my eye as we, delayed
in Birmingham and Crewe, sigh
and turn to newspapers and books
the hidden word; and when you leave
at Wigan without a backward look
taking your rucksack and yawns
I wonder who you were and if
you noticed who I seemed to be.

CYNTHIA KITCHEN *(b. 1947)*

To Lethe on the 8.10

A weak dawn drowns all England under mist;
this train rocks us in its glass cradle
against the track where steel wheels hiss,
a slick of water glimmers on the pylons' cable.

Trees stand out as skeins of blackened wire,
the windows show us staring at our faces;
mist spreads, choking out the sun's ash-fire,
the stations' names christen nameless places.

That young couple are joined hand in hand,
he sleeps against her and she strokes his head;
he wakes to see pale fogs inhale the land,
white grasses that the winter leaves for dead.

The girder bridge flits by like a lantern show,
the river drinks our lights in darkness far below.

GRAHAM MORT *(b. 1955)*

Revenant

The night train almost empty,
She, slumped three seats forward,
Is sleeping when I board, and sleeps on
Till Stafford. I do not wake her.

At midnight, she comes to without a start
And stretching noiselessly,
Shakes a blond comet tail of hair,
Blinks at the mirror-window,
Sniffs, and begins with brushes,
Sponges, sticks and sprays
To make her pale face paler.

That done, she stares about,
Makes gestures of astonished recognition
And squeaks her leathered way
Towards my seat. The patterned tights,
Cloche hat and sequined gloves
Are costume for some play,
In which, currently, I am not cast.

Like a Russian doll
Familiar from common use
I am expeditiously uncased
And all my layered secrets scrutinised.

Yes, I am unpartnered; less rich than heretofore;
Have fewer influential friends
And, in a somewhat undistinguished way,
Am now inclined to baldness.

For a moment, she plays with the jewellery
At her throat, eyes me,
Decides what grip would make
A stranglehold . . . then loses interest.

Parading goodbye teeth
She edges back to bulging briefcase
And a pocket calculator.

Only then I realise I've no idea
What she is doing
Nowadays.

ALAN DAVIS *(b. 1929)*

Girl in a Train

You wear your calm
Like porcelain
Taking cool and fragile care
Not to look at me.

But your reflected self
Mirrored in the window,
Moving through the leafless trees,
Mistily over frosted fields
Blooded with winter sun,
That self regards my reflection
Boldly, steadily.

It is our ghosts who sit
In these substantial seats;
Our honest selves
Kiss in the glass.

FRANK RICKARDS *(b. 1919)*

Travel Notes

(For Frances Nagle)

On the train to Edinburgh
I am reminded
Of your Illuminator poem,

Where Time expands,
Movements are slower than pulse beat,
The pace – *ritardando*.

The girl is beautiful
She takes out manuscript paper,
Stares to distance.

Gradually she places
Quavers, crotchets, phrases,
Rubs them out, begins again.

The people opposite
Record their incomprehension –
Stare, then slide their eyes away.

Three rows down a gang of football fans
Chorus, vulgar-mouth,
Lust after a pretty, waving girl.

Two hundred miles
And what's achieved –
A tracery of breves.

We reach Carlisle
She packs her things,
Puts on her jacket, green peaked cap.

I watch her go
And long to know that wisp of tune
Composed on British Rail.

FRANCES SACKETT *(b. 1948)*

Faintheart in a Railway Train

At nine in the morning there passed a church,
At ten there passed me by the sea,
At twelve a town of smoke and smirch,
At two a forest of oak and birch,
    And then, on a platform, she:

A radiant stranger, who saw not me.
I said, 'Get out to her do I dare?'
But I kept my seat in my search for a plea,
And the wheels moved on. O could it but be
    That I had alighted there!

THOMAS HARDY *(1840–1928)*

The Train

She sat across the train, head flecked
With sleepers leaping up in the sunlight.
So I never spoke, but kept reflecting
How her face would touch the glass and go
And how we had to leave at different stations
Caught together in the moment's journey
And no geometry to bring the lines back
Cross the empty platforms and the waiting rooms
The trains delayed and broken down.

I met her eyes and wished the place
Where trains might be derailed.

KENNETH STEVEN *(b. 1968)*

Travel

The railroad track is miles away,
   And the day is loud with voices speaking,
Yet there isn't a train goes by all day
   But I hear its whistle shrieking.

All night there isn't a train goes by,
   Though the night is still for sleep and dreaming,
But I see its cinders red on the sky
   And hear its engine steaming.

My heart is warm with friends I make,
   And better friends I'll not be knowing;
Yet there isn't a train I wouldn't take,
   No matter where it's going.

EDNA ST VINCENT MILLAY *(1892–1950)*

In the Train

As we rush, as we rush in the Train,
   The trees and the houses go wheeling back,
But the starry heavens above the plain
   Come flying on our track.

All the beautiful stars of the sky,
   The silver doves of the forest of Night,
Over the dull earth swarm and fly,
   Companions of our flight.

We will rush ever on without fear;
   Let the goal be far, the flight be fleet!
For we carry the Heavens with us, dear,
   While the earth slips from our feet!

JAMES THOMSON *(1834–82)*

Trains

1

If ever there was a vehicle for nostalgia

2

Puffing along between heaven and earth

3

There is the carriage of childhood

4

The interview that will dig up your days

5

No such thing as an undecided train

6

Throbbing and slowing. Full tilt. Inch by inch

7

Ears eyes nose hands tongue

8

There is terror of stepping on the wrong train

9

Terror of stepping on the only train.

WILLIAM SCAMMELL *(b. 1939)*

From a Railway Carriage

Faster than fairies, faster than witches,
Bridges and houses, hedges and ditches;
And charging along like troops in a battle
All through the meadows, the horses and cattle:
All of the sights of the hill and the plain
Fly as thick as driving rain;
And, ever again, in the wink of an eye,
Painted stations whistle by.

Here is a child who clambers and scrambles,
All by himself and gathering brambles;
Here is a tramp who stands and gazes
And there is the green for stringing the daisies.
Here is a cart run away in the road
Lumping along with man and load;
And here is a mill and there is a river.
Each a glimpse and gone for ever.

R.L. STEVENSON *(1850–94)*

Waving at Trains

Do people who wave at trains
Wave at the driver, or at the train itself?
Or, do people who wave at trains
Wave at the passengers? Those hurtling strangers,
The unidentifiable flying faces?

They must think we like being waved at.
Children do perhaps, and alone
In a compartment, the occasional passenger
Who is himself a secret waver at trains.
But most of us are unimpressed.

Some even think they're daft.
Stuck out there in a field, grinning.
But our ignoring them, our blank faces,
Even our pulled tongues and up you signs
Come three miles further down the line.

Out of harm's way by then
They continue their walk.
Refreshed and made pure, by the mistaken belief
That their love has been returned,
Because they have not seen it rejected.

It's like God in a way. Another day
Another universe. Always off somewhere.
And left behind, the faithful few,
Stuck out there. Not a care in the world.
All innocence. Arms in the air. Waving.

ROGER McGOUGH (b. 1937)

The Figure in the Doorway
or, On Being Looked at in a Train

The grade surmounted, we were riding high
Through level mountains nothing to the eye
But scrub oak, scrub oak and the lack of earth
That kept the oaks from getting any girth.
But as through the monotony we ran,
We came to where there was a living man.
His great gaunt figure filled his cabin door,
And had he fallen inward on the floor,
He must have measured to the further wall.
But we who passed were not to see him fall.
The miles and miles he lived from anywhere
Were evidently something he could bear.
He stood unshaken, and if grim and gaunt,
It was not necessarily from want.
He had the oaks for heating and for light.
He had a hen, he had a pig in sight.
He had a well, he had the rain to catch.
He had a ten-by-twenty garden patch.
Nor did he lack for common entertainment.
That I assume was what our passing train meant.
He could look at us in our diner eating,
And if so moved uncurl a hand in greeting.

ROBERT FROST *(1874–1963)*

Intercity Animal

... Had to run
hard to catch this train
– Hoarse sensation
from belly to brain
shuddering, juddering
the sou'westerly rain

                     express
stutters to halt amid ploughed
fields – easier to
write now, *hee-haws and
hoots*, I shift to lean
more easily, so do
neighbours, – though city-bound
gent strides

              out of our compartment
and pulls down window
– This compartment all aware
of me scribbling now
suddenly urgent
with electric energy from
another train that shizzes past
  ... *whoosh*: abrupt silence
– Footsteps pass ... down
the corridor – *Cotswold Life*
shiny journal crackles,
embarrassed country girl
scratches at stocking, per-
functory conversation resumes as
train starts up I stop

MICHAEL HOROVITZ *(b. 1935)*

Sassenachs

Me and my best pal (well, she was
till a minute ago) – are off to London.
first trip on an inter-city alone.
When we got on we were the same
kind of excited – jigging on our seats,
staring at everyone. But then,
I remembered I was to be sophisticated.
So when Jenny starts shouting,
'Look at that the land's flat already'
when we are just outside Glasgow
(Motherwell actually) I feel myself flush.
Or even worse, 'Sassenach country!
Wey Hey Hey.' The tartan tammy
sitting proudly on top of her pony;
the tartan scarf swinging like a tail.
The nose pressed to the window.
'England's not so beautiful, is it?'
And we haven't even crossed the border!
And the train's jazzy beat joins her:
Sassenachs sassenachs here we come.
Sassenachs sassenachs Rum Tum Tum
Sassenachs sassenachs how do you do.
SASSENACHS SASSENACHS WE'LL GET YOU!
Then she loses momentum, so out come
the egg mayonnaise sandwiches and
the big bottle of bru. 'My ma's done us proud,'
says Jenny, digging in, munching loud.
The whole train is an egg and I'm inside it.
I try and remain calm; Jenny starts it again,
Sassenachs sassenachs Rum Tum Tum.

Finally we get there: London, Euston;
and the very first person on the platform
gets asked – 'Are you a genuine sassenach?'
I wanted to die, but instead I say, '*Jenny!*'
He replies in that English way –
'I beg your pardon,' and Jenny screams,
'Did you hear that Voice?'
And we both die laughing, clutching
our stomachs at Euston station.

JACKIE KAY *(b. 1961)*

Dawn

(From the train between Bologna
and Milan, second class)

Opposite me two Germans snore and sweat.
  Through sullen swirling gloom we jolt and roar.
We have been here for ever: even yet
  A dim watch tells two hours, two aeons, more
The windows are tight-shut and slimy-wet
  With a night's foetor. There are two hours more;
Two hours to dawn and Milan; two hours yet.
  Opposite me two Germans sweat and snore . . .

One of them wakes, and spits, and sleeps again.
  The darkness shivers. A wan light through the rain
Strikes on our faces, drawn and white. Somewhere
  A new day sprawls; and, inside, the foul air
Is chill, and damp, and fouler than before . . .
  Opposite me two Germans sweat and snore.

RUPERT BROOKE *(1887–1915)*

The Loneliness of an Empty Railway Carriage

The City dirt,
The sharp smell of burnt oil,
Hang on this train;

Empty and swept
It slides its old-fashioned rump
Through the greening night;

From a tall nail
A long yellow sheet
Rocks in its plastic jive.

The floors are cold
With dull mosaics
Of permanent stains.

No other life
Shares in this carriage ride
With me,

While I watch
In the dusk the closing in
Of bereaved upholstery.

Knowing there's light
Somewhere outside
Where the table is laid,

Or where cattle stand
With good faces
In the mist of a spring meadow.

LOTTE KRAMER *(b. 1923)*

The Spitfire on the Northern Line

Harry was an uncle. I saw him twice.
Both times he was a sailor home from war.
First, he arrived one morning, thumped the door,
Annoying old Ma Brown on the second floor,
And brought me two string-bags click-full of marbles.
In the grey light of that wartime dawn we lay
On the cold lino, rumbling zig-zag balls
Of colour to all corners of the room,
Until Ma Brown banged up at us with her broom.
I felt like a god in heaven, playing with thunder.
The second time, we went by Underground
To see his mother, my grandma. In all
That packed and rocking tube-train, down we sat
Together on the dirty wooden slats
Between the feet of passengers, and began
To build a Spitfire. He would send me off
Toddling with tininess against the sway
Of the train to fetch a propeller, then the wheels,
While like a Buddha crosslegged, all in blue,
He sat and bashed a nail or sank a screw.
And before the eyes of all, a Spitfire grew
And finally (a stop before the Angel)
He cried 'It's finished!' and the whole coachful
Shouted 'Hooray!'
                                    Never, never again
Did I see Harry. Somewhere he was killed
And they slipped his body softly to the sea.
Thousands died that war. Most, like Harry,
Not distinguished by the enemies gunned down,
But remembered by some child.
                                    I see it still
That Spitfire on the Northern Line, nose-up,
Blotched with its camouflage, and gleaming bright,
And all those faces laughing with delight.

BRIAN JONES *(b. 1938)*

Sleeping Compartment

I don't like this, being carried sideways
through the night. I feel wrong and helpless – like
a timber broadside in a fast stream.

Such a way of moving may suit
that odd snake the sidewinder
in Arizona: but not me in Perthshire.

I feel at right angles to everything,
a cross grain in existence. – It scrapes
the top of my head, my footsoles.

To forget outside is no help either –
then I become a blockage
in the long gut of the train.

I try to think I am a through-the-looking-glass
mountaineer bivouacked
in a ledge five feet high.

It's no good. I go sidelong.
I rock sideways . . . I draw in my feet
to let Aviemore pass.

NORMAN MacCAIG *(b. 1910–96)*

Slow Movement

Waking, he found himself in a train, andante,
With wafers of early sunlight blessing the unknown fields
And yesterday cancelled out, except for yesterday's papers
    Huddling under the seat.

It is still very early, this is a slow movement;
The viola-player's hand like a fish in a glass tank
Rises, remains quivering, darts away
    To nibble invisible weeds.

Great white nebulae lurch against the window
To deploy across the valley, the children are not yet up
To wave us on – we pass without spectators,
    Braiding a voiceless creed.

And the girl opposite, name unknown, is still
Asleep and the colour of her eyes unknown
Which might be wells of sun or moons of wish
    But it is still very early.

The movement ends, the train has come to a stop
In buttercup fields, the fiddles are silent, the whole
Shoal of silver tessellates the aquarium
    Floor, not a bubble rises . . .

And what happens next on the programme we do not know,
If, the red line topped on the gauge, the fish will go mad in the
    tank
Accelerando con forza, the sleeper open her eyes
    And, so doing, open ours.

LOUIS MacNEICE *(1907–63)*

The Night Journey

Hands and lit faces eddy to a line;
    The dazed last minutes click; the clamour dies.
Beyond the great-swung arc o' the roof, divine,
    Night, smoky-scarv'd, with thousand coloured eyes

Glares the imperious mystery of the way.
    Thirsty for dark, you feel the long-limbed train
Throb, stretch, thrill motion, slide, pull out and sway,
    Strain for the far, pause, draw to strength again . . .

– As a man, caught by some great hour, will rise,
    Slow-limbed, to meet the light or find his love;
And, breathing long, with staring sightless eyes,
    Hands out, head back, agape and silent, move

Sure as a flood, smooth as a vast wind blowing;
    And, gathering power and godhead as he goes,
Unstumbling, unreluctant, strong, unknowing,
    Borne by a will not his, that lifts, that grows,

Sweep into darkness, triumphing to his goal,
    Out of the fire, out of the little room! . . .
– There is an end appointed, O my soul!
    Crimson and green the signals burn. The gloom

Is hung with steam's fantastic livid streamers,
    Lost into God, as lights in light, we fly,
Grown one with will, end-drunken huddled dreamers.
    The white lights roar; the sounds of the world die;

And lips and laughter are forgotten things.
    Speed sharpens; grows. Into the night, and on,
The strength and splendour of our purpose swings.
    The lamps fade; and the stars. We are alone.

RUPERT BROOKE *(1887–1915)*

The Space Age of the Train

Our craft leaves the launch pad,
moves along its steel trajectory,

finds escape velocity and is off
to shudder through space and time.

We move quickly along the aisles
in search of food and diversion,

pull open the airlocks and enter
the next compartmentalised world.

Weightless and buffeted from wall
to wall, we hang on to the plastic

pre-packed rations; a dehydrated
sandwich and a can of warm beer.

A robot voice prickly with static
announces our mission termination.

We decelerate, prior to re-entry
and come down to Earth with a jolt.

Our suitcases fill with gravity,
as we stagger to the exit points

and clamber out of the shuttle.
Aliens greet us. Their message is

unintelligible over loud speakers.
The air is barely breathable here,

but the platform we are walking on
seems capable of supporting life.

CHRIS WOODS *(b. 1950)*

Trains

I like to feel on trains
That I was only there for half the ride
Not at its start nor at its bitter end
But getting on at Derby, off at Leeds
And going casually about my business
Whilst other suckers slog on up to Scotland.

Travel for two hours can be neat and conscious
More than that and things start to get messy.

MANDY SUTTER *(b. 1957)*

Train Journey

Wet slag-yards
Wet slate-roofs
Grey as the train slides
Easily
Sleazily by
Like an expensive snake.
And I
Warmly digesting
In the sleek interior
Will let no woman's weariness,
No fouled tinker's ground,
Nothing that squats
In the landscape outside
Scar this skin-smooth hour;
Nothing exterior
Disturb this composure;
My wounds wait me
At the end of the line.

F. LOVELL *(b. 1938)*

Was it You at Warrington?

'Was that Derek waiting on the platform?'
One of them spluttered, the train slowing down,
her mother and sister had seen him too,
a Preston friend at Warrington of all places
but it sent them homing like unhampered pigeons
'Down Fishergate, over the bridge
and we'll soon be home then.
No more waiting and changing.'

Eleven, twelve the older girl
was for walking back down the train
to see if it really was him
but their mother – 'No, when we get to Preston
we'll look for him on the station.'
'And if we see him' the young one fluttered (a moment later
all of them laughing) 'we can ask him
Was it you at Warrington?'

So as the train gained speed
There was nothing for the girls but to watch
the swelps of rosebay willowherb blurring
beds of pink over green; the sunset
rippled a fireweed light into their eyes
more beautiful each mile for home
till whether or not it was him at Warrington,
it was never going to be them at Preston.

DICK WILKINSON *(b. 1926)*

Travelling

'Peckham Rye, Loughborough, Elephant, St Paul's.'
Every morning the porter bawls.
The train grinds out . . . and I gaze on lots
Of sad back gardens and chimney-pots,
Factory stacks and smoky haze
Showering smuts on the close-packed ways.
And the train jolts on and twists and crawls . . .
'Peckham Rye, Loughborough, Elephant, St Paul's.'

But, trapped and prisoned as I may be,
I lift a latch and my thoughts go free,
And once again I am running down
On a winding track from a Cornish town
And I dream the names of the stations through –
'Moorswater, Causeland, Sandplace, Looe.'

An ancient engine with puff nigh gone,
Drags a couple of coaches on
Close where a stream runs all the way
Muttering music night and day;
There isn't a porter about at all
To spoil the peace with a raucous bawl,
But a kind old guard to see me through,
Give me a ticket and take it too.
The line twists down through patches sweet
Of soft green pasture and waving wheat
And the stream spreads out to a river wide
Where ships creep up at the turn of tide,
Till a tangle of spars on a blue sky spun
Gives me the sign of the journey done,
And I stand contented on the quay
And hear the surging song of the sea.

So runs the dreamlike journey through,
'Moorswater, Causeland, Sandplace, Looe'; –
But every morning the porter bawls,
'Peckham Rye, Loughborough, Elephant, St Paul's.'

BERNARD MOORE *(b. 1873–c. 1920)*

Train Journey: Eller Fields

The first glimpses were between trees –
Scattered fields hanging in distances: here,
Humping (ominous, animal) on the horizon; there,
Discarded scarf hugging the shoulder of the hill;
Or flashing pocket handkerchief, nothing smudged
Or blurred, but hard-edged, clean; or a slice
Of lemon-rind, of kids' painted suns smiling high
In corners. The images spawned.

I surmised, at first, that they were daffodils –
Too dense, much too-even-spread for dandelions –
But this wasn't Lincolnshire, for the land rose
And gave, rose and gave again. Not dandelions.
Not daffodils. What then?

Curiosity aroused, and sensing how distances
Compromise appearances, I saw that parallels
Of green striped the fields where sowing-machine
Had tracked, and where it turned had scored vast
Noughtsandcrosses boards upon the land. I thought
Of Mondrian's *Broadway Boogie-Woogie* with its flashy plashes
Of primaries, its jazzy symmetries, sunshine brassiness,
And how it moved, how the painting moved. But how
The fields had moved – nearer, near, their acid keenness
Intensifying in surprising violence, blanking-out
The carriage-glass in floods of citrine, the oh-so-small,
So fleshly-delicate scales of oil-seed rape. (Just calculate
The myriad-teeming petal-heads, the insurgencies of growth –
The mind reeled, how it reeled.) Till a young girl pealed,
'Eller. Mum. Eller. Sun's fell asleep.'
And the fields flashed laughing back, like the child's incisive
    gaze.

ROGER ELKIN   *(b. 1943)*

A Mind's Journey to Diss

Dear Mary,
    Yes, it will be bliss
To go with you by train to Diss,
Your walking shoes upon your feet;
We'll meet, my sweet, at Liverpool Street,
That levellers we may be reckoned
Perhaps we'd better travel second;
Or, lest reporters on us burst,
Perhaps we'd better travel first.
Above the chimney-pots we'll go
Through Stepney, Stratford-atte-Bow
And out to where the Essex marsh
Is filled with houses new and harsh
Till, Witham pass'd, the landscape yields
On left and right to widening fields,
Flint church-towers sparkling in the light,
Black beams and weather-boarding white,
Cricket-bat willows silvery green
And elmy hills with brooks between,
Maltings and saltings, stack and quay
And, somewhere near, the grey North Sea;
Then further gentle undulations
With lonelier and less frequent stations,
Till in the dimmest place of all
The train slows down into a crawl
And stops in silence ... Where is this?
Dear Mary Wilson, this is Diss.

JOHN BETJEMAN *(1906–84)*

Reply to the Laureate

Dear John,
    Yes, it is perfect bliss
To go with you by train to Diss!
Beneath a soft East Anglian rain
We chug across the ripening plain
Where daisies stand among the hay;
We come to Diss on Market Day,
And cloth-capped farmers sit around,
Their booted feet firm on the ground;
They talk of sheep, the price of corn;
We find the house where I was born –
How small it seems! for memory
Has played its usual trick on me.
The chapel where my father preached
Can now, alas, only be reached
By plunging through the traffic's roar;
We go in by the Gothic door
To meet, within the vestry dim,
An old man who remembers him.
Now, as we stroll beside the Mere,
Reporters suddenly appear;
You draw a crowd of passers-by
Whilst I gaze blandly at the sky;
An oak-beamed refuge then we find,
The scones are good, the waitress kind;
Old ladies, drinking cups of tea,
Discuss their ailments cheerfully.
Across the window-ledge we lean
To look down on the busy scene,
And there, among the booths below,
Fat jolly babies kick and crow
As, wheeled by mothers young and fair,
They jolt around the Market Square.
School-children, dragging tired feet
Trail home along the winding street.
The church clock strikes a mellow chime

Just to remind us of the time;
We climb the hill as daylight fails,
The train comes panting up the rails,
And as the summer dusk comes down,
We travel slowly back to town.
What day could be more sweet than this,
Dear John, the day we came to Diss?

MARY WILSON (b. 1916)

Deganwy Villanelle

I only remember long days of happy summer
Penny daisies brightening dusty verges
Tick-a-ta thump tick-a-ta thump of the Llandudno train.

Jewels of golden gorse and bird's foot trefoil
On the springy turf over the Castle humps,
I only remember long days of happy summer.

The tiny beach beyond the railway crossing
High signal box with footings on the strand
Tick-a-ta thump tick-a-ta thump of the Llandudno train.

Hot sun on bare backs, sand between sticky toes
Scorching under tender soles
I only remember long days of happy summer.

Grit in the bite of sandwiches and pears
A bottle of cool white milk to drink
Tick-a-ta thump tick-a-ta thump of the Llandudno train.

Ankles aching in froth of freezing water
Wheeling and keening of incessant gulls
I only remember long days of happy summer
Tick-a-ta thump tick-a-ta thump of the Llandudno train.

MARY BRETT (b. 1929)

Transpennine

The centre circle has grown long months into the season
but the ten-yard box is mud; and we're past
where little bays of rock admit a tide of stone –
hard not to keep seeing the hills as a sea; nearer,
the corrugated roofs of outhouses undulate the light
from a village that is clean, grey, clean.
A woman with B.O. bores a five year old out of the Beano
and the lane up to Slaithwaite Bandroom goes by – one in three,
imagine carrying a tuba up there! – followed by a starburst
of rooks at 70 mph until we brake until
we all but stop beside a glass lock; and are
trapped by the reflection of a sky. The canal is our height
chasing, when we begin again, like a dog through the valley
at our side, faithful, reliable and no use. Beyond it
where trade has slackened are car park poles
for show jumping, half a dozen strides apart. The woman
talks to me and half the carriage, while the child
grips her knuckles on the rolled-up comic
and beats time. The houses and installations
are gothic as are the black silhouettes of cows
and the station master, his blurred identikit face,
hopeless on an all-stations platform . . .
A seed drill this first day of November and a church tower
each in their way point the finger at God,
who responds with a line of rain and sunshine:
a rainbow over Stalybridge, where, if I were
visiting you, I would change. But I am going
to Manchester, Manchester where we have never been
and our faces fit: Simon, Anita, Michael:
down they step from offices into everyday drizzle, raising
their collars and light umbrellas.

PETER SANSOM *(b. 1958)*

The Old Great Western Line

Flashing past my carriage windows,
On the old Great Western Line,
Engine steam the rushing wind blows
Half obscures this land of mine.
We have come from Cardiff Central,
On our journey up the Taff,
And we're bound for Merthyr Tydfil
On a rising, curving, graph.

We will call at Cardiff Queen Street,
Llandaff, Radyr and Taffs Well.
Then at both Treforest stations
Looking like the gates of hell.
The sluggish river putrefies,
With foul industrial waste,
As our locomotive bustles by
With quite indecorous haste.

We will change our train at Ponty,
This one goes to Aberdare,
But they're bound to have one handy,
By the time that we reach there.
We will look down where the road drops,
To the town below the bridge,
We will cast our eyes past roof tops,
To that Needle on the ridge.

We will climb the wooded gradient,
To our stop at Quakers Yard,
And then onward to Mount Pleasant
Past the hillsides torn and scarred.
The Merthyr Vale (for Aberfan)
Where pit wheel starkly spins,
And slag heaps poise to wait for man
To lose what coal dust wins.

We have come from Cardiff Central
On our journey up the Taff.

And we're bound for Merthyr Tydfil,
Through the Halt at Pentrebach.
Flashing past my carriage windows
From that childhood world of mine,
Come the images that time blows
Down the old Great Western Line.

RAY HARMAN *(b. 1922)*

Journey – London to Cambridge

What reality exists in this, to sit
in a mechanised glow-worm, creeping
out from the concrete forest
under a dark December dawn?
Strange, yet less than strange
to see these passing homes,
their safety of nestled stone
and security of lights in breakfast windows,
sped and gone,
sped and gone like meteorites,
an unreal backcloth spun off the reel of time
with no re-wind.

What vitality exists in this, to see
the houses like frosted bun-loaves
line the shelves of winter fields
where charcoaled whiteness gleams?
And there they huddle in the dawn
as neighbour trees in copses
rooted, drained by a night network.
Sad, yet less than sad
to know we flit
small burdened sparrows
drawn by light into a great hall
in and out
in and out of windows with no glass.

GLADYS MARY COLES *(b. 1942)*

First Train to Devil's Bridge

Eight I was that first trip on Y Lein Fach –
A family outing on the little train.
How small the engine – a pet one you could pat –
Dark green shining, brass plates gleaming.
I stroked it and it waggled its whistle and tooted!
We climbed into the open-air coach
And at the green flag's wave, jolted on our way.

At first we jogged along the valley floor;
At the level-crossing in Llanbadarn
I waved to everyone and everyone waved back –
Then began the climb. 'They've
put another lump of coal on' said my mother,
And I hung out to see
The plucky little engine snaking round a corner,
Huffing and chuffing out great clouds of smoke
As it thought its way through oaks halfway up the mountain.
I tried in vain to grab souvenir acorns
Before we left the woods behind
To see views again across the valley.

'Look at the Stag!!' yelled everyone and pointed –
I stared at the bare rocky space amid the greenery
And watched it magic into shape until,
Bent double, we disappeared round another bend
And I could wave triumphant at the last slowcoach.
With victory shriek and cloud of self-important steam
Our model engine halted among rhododendrons,
And out I tumbled intent on waterfalls and picnics.

After an afternoon amid dark pools and high rocks
The evening journey back seemed all downhill to me –
Chin on hands I rushed into the sun
Round precipice rim and towering crag,
The engine in its element, knowing it could,
Whistling like mad and sending smuts through every window.
I thought it wanted supper, just like me –
A good wash and a long cool drink
A quiet time to recollect, then happy dreams.

MARY MESTECKY (b. 1938)

Aberdeen Train

Rubbing a glistening circle
on the steamed-up window I framed
a pheasant in a field of mist.
The sun was a great red thing somewhere low,
Struggling with the milky scene. In the furrows
a piece of glass winked into life,
hypnotized the silly dandy; we
hooted past him with his head cocked,
contemplating a bottle-end.
And this was the last of October,
A Chinese moment in the Mearns.

EDWIN MORGAN (b. 1920)

Excursion

The train beats the track
like a tin drum; whistle hooting,
farmhouses bobbing on streams of green.
A warm breeze from an open window
played with her hair, sweeping down
a silky mesh across her sleeping face.

Then, a new rhythm rocking to sea –
diddle-de-dee
diddle-de-dee
and I, too, fell to dreams
of unicorns and brindled cows,
woke to catch bold brush strokes,
a blazing fox in the sun-soaked field
where angels scythed golden wheat.

Gathering speed we flooded estuaries
and the sky was all watery and alive
with dolphin dances till a tunnel
swallowed us whole – belched up
and beached mother and I
at Brighton Station. From the top
of the street, the sea was high as houses,
and hand in hand sleepily
we went down and down,

the sun melting the sky
to a froth of boiling milk.
She lay in the blue-striped
deck-chair, eyes closed,
and the beach stones clacked
and clagged her indifference all day.
And she was my friend no more.
I sulked at the sea's edge, pushing
back waves with my scraggy feet.

SUSAN SAUNDERS *(b. 1944)*

Ghost Train

It was an undertaking.
Corner seat, booked in advance,
back to the engine,
luncheon basket ordered
(chicken and ham,
lettuce like frosty mornings,
crusted rolls),
cologne at hand,
lace hanky for the smuts,
a snug, light rug
and sixpences for tips.

Much talk of connections,
fears that things might be
difficult at Crewe
(where a man hanged himself
and who can wonder?).
God-speeds and Give-my-loves –

Bustle – a slam of doors,
obsequious porters
pocketing their pelf,
the glimpse of a green flag.

No count-down but a
pterodactyl scream
slices the day.
Hissing, the jointed snake
jerks into life,
grumbles and thumps,
gains power,
achieves its rhythm,
moves irrevocably
forward into the past.

MEG SEATON *(1907–86)*

Broadening the Mind

If I had read my book on the train
between Manchester and Greenfield
outlining supply side economics
I would have missed the following:
rows of railway arch entrepreneurs
doors bolted against the bank's final word
the girl across repairing the red pout
her boyfriend had damaged in three tunnels,
weathered ghosts of gable-end adverts,
A Cambridge University sweatshirt
with 'Fat Chance' stencilled across it,
two cemeteries one real one auto
allotments overgrown with the latest
out-of-town big shed architecture,
from the estate spreading down to the line
too-good-to-be true garden escapes
easily outclassed by the foxgloves
steepling above the grass everywhere;
the probably over-qualified conductor
ending his list of halts with 'et al',
three clumps of toadflax at Stalybridge
rooted in ballast between the lines
with only diesel stains for sustenance,
soccer graffiti on a bridge
that must have needed a twenty-foot arm,
a view of Mossley's backside
veined with parasitic plumbing,
and thoughts about what I might have seen
if I had over-run my stop
and carried on not reading.

DENNIS TRAVIS *(b. 1930)*

From the Train

From the train at dawn, on ploughland, frost
Blue-white in the shadow of a wood.
Oh, you again, of all moods soonest lost
And most elusive and least understood.
What should I call you? Vision? Empathy?
Elation's tunnel? Worm-hold of rejoicing?
Some bliss of childhood, reasonless and free,
The secret microcosms . . . What a thing
To have no name for, yet to live for, these
Curious contentments under all,
These moments of a planet: weathers, trees –
What dreams, what intimations, fern-seed small,
Are buried in our days, that we must find
And recognise, and lose, and leave behind?

DAVID SUTTON *(b. 1944)*

Commuter Train

Near Cricklewood, where the joined houses show
their shabby backs to railway lines beneath,
a glance while slowing down before the station
revealed a naked figure in a window, gleaming.

A youth, quite nude, stood close against the glass –
not facing me, but inwards to the room.
The glimpse was slight, engendering surmise.
How odd and rare and strangely disconcerting!

Was he an exhibitionist poseur
giving the passing passengers a frisson?
Or posing for a class, or merely dressing?
Was it a fantasy – had I been dreaming?

Monotonous commuting takes me past
the lines of houses, looking much the same.
But never once again have I encountered
the sight of that young man – so bare, so gleaming.

BARBARA BALCH *(b. 1917)*

Vanishing Point

These suburbs could break your heart;
at dusk, or under a heavy sky,
their curtains are open and life carries on
inside yellow rooms.

Plastic toys left out in yards,
a blue formica table, faded;
mattresses, a fridge, a line of washing,
children waving as we travel past some fields.

I pick up my pen to write something
and fight the shaking of the train
to shape my letters, but still my writing
is an old lady's, maybe my granny's,

though it wasn't travelling
that crabbed her hand or made her pen
dance in directions of its own,
yet she noticed how the speed kept on increasing

until the foreground hurled itself towards her
and the houses, trees, fields were a blur
and by the time the children saw her waving
she'd passed us by.

CAROL SHERGOLD *(b. 1960)*

To a Fat Lady Seen from the Train

O why do you walk through the fields in gloves,
    Missing so much and so much?
O fat white woman whom nobody loves,
Why do you walk through the fields in gloves,
When the grass is soft as the breast of doves
    And shivering-sweet to the touch?
O why do you walk through the fields in gloves,
    Missing so much and so much?

FRANCES CORNFORD *(1886–1960)*

To Frances Cornford

(From a fat lady in the fields)

O why do you gawk from the train and taunt,
    Missing so much and so much?
For I am off on an amorous jaunt.
    Why do you gawk from the train and taunt?
I shall meet my love in our meadow haunt
    And discard my gloves at his touch.
O why do you gawk from the train and taunt,
    Missing so much and so much?

JENNY MORRIS *(b. 1940)*

By the Way

Years ago the train stopped somewhere, waiting
in the wings of a drab town. What the plot was,
where we were going, I don't remember.
It was brick country, flat and undefined.
Sunshine that morning; the sky bluish;
clouds piled at a far edge like old snow.
Round us, a cinder desert where coarse grass
hung on in tufts. People refolded papers,
keeping their elbows close, and stared out
at the last slick of building. Over the fence
corner to corner on the end house but three
in thick dribbling letters: WELCOME HOME GEORGE.

Clocks started again and we moved, stiffly,
qui, qui, towards supposed destinations.
Women picked up magazines: qui venit:
wanting to know what happened. Dictus qui
dictus benedictus and round the block
in nomine in nomine steps George looking taller
and we know that somehow after all these years
there's a denouement, everyone's in,
kettle boiling, duffel bag in the hall.
We're moving now, domini domini domini
and the dog's running around grinning and crying
in the grief of catharsis because George is back.

M.R. PEACOCKE (b. 1930)

115

In the Dome Car

The train, as if departure were a state-
Secret, pulls out without a sound. I glance
Up from *The Globe and Mail* surprised to see
Through the dome car's dull window, Canada
Lurching quietly by. *Find the dome car,*
You said to me. *You'll see it all from there.*

And so I do. Or think I do. At first,
The Bow River, surface of china blue,
Indigo-coloured water squeezing through;
The rail-cars straightening in line ahead.
Giacometti trees like naked men
Stand, sky-high, in a littleness of snow;
Adverts for Honda, holidays (*Try us
Ski Jasper*); hunks of rock; the red Dutch barn
Recurring like a decimal; a thin
Smear of gold-leaf that is the coming corn.

In ice-edged light the train moves cautiously
Above a toy village, a clip of black
And white Indian ponies, a tepee
Hoisted beside a brake of pointed sticks.
A bridge hurries to meet us; spills across
A frozen lake. A car parked on the ice,
In shifting light, glitters a mile from shore.
We gape at it. But what I see is you
Walking the long nave of the train-station,
Never turning. *You'll see it all from there.*

We rush the stone horizon. At the last
Moment the mountains part; admit us to
Indian country, where the patient snow
Refuses the year's passage, scars the floor
Of a pale valley; lies in wait no more.

CHARLES CAUSLEY *(b. 1917)*

Natural Break

I'd drudged away a decade's paperwork –
A bluntening human shuttle still intent
On getting there and getting back along
Relentless rails – and never been content
As suddenly I was the other day
With time spent on the journey. The train,
An earlier emptier one, had stopped mid-way
Between two stations, windows downed for air
Against a sheer bruise-coloured cutting-wall.
(Seen at speed, it had been a mere blue blur.)
'Look at the plants,' a woman said 'All
Growing: how on earth do they keep hold?'

The dingy carriage had converted to
A room, with spotlit microscopic view
Of a hanging garden. Knapweed and hawkweed
Shared with ferns and willow-herb and mortared joints
And (caught in closer focus) crisp brick flakes
Flicked out for rootspace. From the bank above,
Of birch and cushion-grass, long trailers hung
Drawing from richer soil – the briars, swung
By years of trains. 'Look at those blackberries!'
The same old woman said. The sunbaked bricks
Had ripened them a month ahead, tempting as cherries
But unreachable: or so I thought at first.

I arched outside to check the lights for time
Then, walking to another window, hooked
The nearest truss across the gap – and plucked
The small warm weights into my palm
Four fruits were enough: two for the old couple;
And the other lightly dusted ones I ate,
Crushing out their juice as the signal cleared
From red to steady amber in the heat.

PETER WALTON (b. 1936)

Daniel

sets up a plastic train set
on the table of a train
travelling from Tiverton to Bristol.

'Wind up the engine Mum.
Look it's frightened the donkey
by the bridge.

When this treatment's finished
can we go to London?'

She helps him on with his sweater
fastens the buttons at the neck

settles a green cap on his bald head.

PATRICIA POGSON *(b. 1944)*

Corner Seat

Suspended in a moving night
The face in the reflected train
Looks at first sight as self-assured
As your own face – But look again:
Windows between you and the world
Keep out the cold, keep out the fright;
Then why does your reflection seem
So lonely in the moving night?

LOUIS MacNEICE *(1907–63)*

FOUR

Oh, Mr Porter!

THE MEN OF IRON

Labourers on the Settle–Carlisle Railway

At sixpence an hour,
with pick and shovel,
spit, foul mouth and sweat,
they built this railway
over a land the glaciers
booby-trapped with boulder clay
to be blasted like rock,
ladled out like soup in buckets.

They lived in tents on Blea Moor, where snow
lay two months on the backs of hill sheep,
plodged four times a day through kneedeep slime
to get from meat to work and back again,
lodged on open fellsides in shanty towns
they called Sebastopol, Jericho, Jerusalem,
Belgravia – or plain Tunnel Huts.

Had little taste for charity,
for concerts, Penny Readings, lay preachers,
Quaker ladies, bobbies, excisemen.
Spent their leisure swilling down booze
or in fist fights. Once hit the headlines
dancing naked at the Hill Inn
with Mary Ann Lee, and so wrote themselves
into a short footnote in history.

They died of TB, smallpox, dysentery;
in chance encounters with engines;
in frenzied brawls with anyone to hand.
They fell from cranes or under cartwheels;
were blown to bits by dynamite;
drowned in tunnels, in flash floods,
in ditches, paralytic with drink.
Hanged themselves from bridges.

Are now remembered, if at all, by nicknames:
Nobby Scandalous, Tiger, Gipsy, Punch.
Their bones lie in unmarked graves;
their memorials those crumbling viaducts
and ghost stations along a line
gentlemen in London with soft hands
would close to save on candle ends.

JOHN WARD (b. 1915)

To the Late Thomas Sharp

Could but this great ancestor rise again
Now to enjoy the presence of his men
His soul thus lighted with a holy flame
Methinks 'twould burst in some such following strain:-
'Is this the Atlas that mine eyes now see
Which was an infant dandled on my knee?
Is this the harvest of the seeds I've sown
The fruits of which now dignify the town?
Is this the Atlas with her flag unfurled
That's now become the wonder of the world?

Go on, great Atlas, and thou must prevail
Whilst yet these engines ply upon the rail
Breathe forth pure science from thine inmost soul
To commercialise the world from pole to pole.
Go on, proud Atlas, for thy glory shines,
Thou greatest, mightiest, victor of the lines, –
May future sons of science find a fold
And spread the fame of Atlas to the world.
And may this theme vibrate your honest hearts
Long live the name and Atlas firm of Sharps.'

MR MELLOR (c. 1800–70)

The Spiritual Railway

Epitaph on a tombstone at Ely Cathedral
(To two navvies who died on Christmas Eve 1845
on the Ely to Peterborough Line.)

The line to Heaven by Christ was made
With heavenly truth the rails are laid
From Earth to Heaven the Line extends
To Life Eternal where it ends

Repentance is the Station then
Where Passengers are taken in
No Fee for them is there to pay
For Jesus is himself the way

God's Word is the first Engineer
It points the way to Heaven so clear,
Through tunnels dark and dreary here
It does the way to Glory steer.

God's Love the Fire, his Truth the Steam,
Which drives the Engine and the Train
All you who would to Glory ride,
Must come to Christ, in him abide

In First and Second, and Third Class,
Repentance, Faith and Holiness
You must the way to Glory gain
Or you with Christ will not remain

Come then poor Sinners, now's the time
At any Station on the Line
If you'll repent and turn from Sin
The train will stop and take you in

ANON.

Getting on on the Railways

There's few but me's plain goods-porter here.
Soon as you've to read labels to know where
to hump the stuff they're tied to, grade goes up:
special abilities. 'Sides, there's other things.

Take the motormen, allus arguing
with the men who load the trailers for their rounds,
how all's in the wrong order to pull off.
Both once were graded checkers. Motormen
got together, stuck out for how they must
get made up senior checkers so they can
bollocks the loaders, call them every name
under the sun like they do anyway,
but by rights, for stacking trailers wrong,
Next the loaders found out that the forms
they list the goods on aren't straightforward forms,
oh no, they're multiple, carbons and all.
That entitled them to upgrading too.
So the motormen are back at square one. It'll
go on till they're all station managers.
They'd still waste half the morning arguing.

Another case: old Greg who checks out stock
in the Order Shed, he's not allowed to lift,
that's why they gave him that job. Can't hold owt,
poor old Gregory, not even his beer,
really shouldn't be working, no, the only
place for him is six foot under. Well,
he got so much wrong counting cartons out
they made him up a grade to give him an
increased sense of responsibility.
So now he draws more doing more things wrong.
Wrecking the bloody railways'd take him to
the big boss seat. He'd not be first, at that.

SEAMUS HEANEY (b. 1939)

Skimbleshanks: The Railway Cat

There's a whisper down the line at 11.39
When the Night Mail's ready to depart,
Saying 'Skimble where is Skimble has he gone to hunt the
    thimble?
We must find him or the train can't start.'
All the guards and all the porters and the stationmaster's
    daughters
They are searching high and low,
Saying 'Skimble where is Skimble for unless he's very nimble
Then the Night Mail just can't go.'
At 11.42 then the signal's overdue
And the passengers are frantic to a man –
Then Skimble will appear and he'll saunter to the rear:
He's been busy in the luggage van!
    He gives one flash of his glass-green eyes
        And the signal goes 'All Clear!'
    And we're off at last for the northern part
        Of the Northern Hemisphere!

You may say that by and large it is Skimble who's in charge
Of the Sleeping Car Express.
From the driver and the guards to the bagmen playing cards
He will supervise them all, more or less.
Down the corridor he paces and examines all the faces
Of the travellers in the First and in the Third;
He establishes control by a regular patrol
And he'd know at once if anything occurred.
He will watch you without winking and he sees what you are
    thinking
And it's certain that he doesn't approve
Of the hilarity and riot, so the folk are very quiet
When Skimble is about and on the move.
    You can play no pranks with Skimbleshanks!
        He's a Cat that cannot be ignored;
    So nothing goes wrong on the Northern Mail
        When Skimbleshanks is aboard.

Oh it's very pleasant when you have found your little den
With your name written up on the door.
And the berth is very neat with a newly folded sheet
And there's not a speck of dust on the floor.
There is every sort of light – you can make it dark or bright;
There's a button that you turn to make a breeze.
There's a funny little basin you're supposed to wash your face
   in
And a crank to shut the window if you sneeze.
Then the guard looks in politely and will ask you very
   brightly
'Do you like your morning tea weak or strong?'
But Skimble's just behind him and was ready to remind him.
For Skimble won't let anything go wrong.
   And when you creep into your cosy berth
      And pull up the counterpane,
   You ought to reflect that it's very nice
   To know that you won't be bothered by mice –
   You can leave all that to the Railway Cat,
      The Cat of the Railway Train!

In the watches of the night he is always fresh and bright;
Every now and then he has a cup of tea
With perhaps a drop of Scotch while he's keeping on the
   watch,
Only stopping here and there to catch a flea.
You were fast asleep at Crewe and so you never knew
That he was walking up and down the station;
You were sleeping all the while he was busy at Carlisle,
Where he greets the stationmaster with elation.
But you saw him at Dumfries, where he summons the police
If there's anything they ought to know about:
When you get to Gallowgate there you do not have to wait –
For Skimbleshanks will help you to get out!
      He gives you a wave of his long brown tail
         Which says: 'I'll see you again!
      You'll meet without fail on the Midnight Mail
         The Cat of the Railway Train.'

T.S. ELIOT (1888–1965)

Diesel Driver

A six foot windscreen and a bench of gadgets,
easy as wafting a kid's three wheeler.
Left lever off and let her gather,
feel her pull, strong, her rhythm settle,
check with wristed time, make the straight, faster –
Gobowen, Ruabon, Wrexham, Chester.

Flush a thatch of fantails, a hawk from hover,
send a linesman skittling for banked cover,
make the butterfly-tossed bay willow rustle,
the corn-set poppies flinch and wrestle –
give an extra toot if you see your sister –
Gobowen, Ruabon, Wrexham, Chester.

Far off those lines must surely meet –
like looking up the straddled legs of a giant.
They never do. Now it's curve, meander,
slack off a bit, watch points.
Then the first houses, a tightening cluster –
Gobowen, Ruabon, Wrexham, Chester.

Wail for slow down, shush to a stop,
doors clacked open, porters' hustle.
'Trust the Lord With All Your Heart' on placard.
Llangollen coracles, trolleys tipped,
a last sweaty passenger in a swearing fluster –
Gobowen, Ruabon, Wrexham, Chester.

Then off again, hummed past the signal
– a thoughtful heron angling its red-white beak –
under a leapfrog come and go of bridges,
skirting the old sandpit, the men fishing
round where the woods lean over, the jackdaws muster –
Gobowen, Ruabon, Wrexham, Chester.

Trim as a trout in a Sunday suit,
snug as a grape in a Guernsey greenhouse,
who's to sigh for the steamy past?
No more gritty eyes, blown caps, cracked faces –
not even an oil-tarred shirt, a footplate blister –
Gobowen, Ruabon, Wrexham, Chester.

GEOFFREY HOLLOWAY *(b.1918)*

Morning Express

Along the wind-swept platform, pinched and white,
The travellers stand in pools of wintry light,
Offering themselves to morn's long, slanting arrows.
The train's due; porters trundle laden barrows.
The train steams in, volleying resplendent clouds
Of sun-blown vapour. Hither and about,
Scared people hurry, storming the doors in crowds.
The officials seem to waken with a shout,
Resolved to hoist and plunder; some to the vans
Leap; others rumble the milk in gleaming cans.

Boys, indolent-eyed, from baskets leaning back,
Question each face; a man with a hammer steals
Stooping from coach to coach; with clang and clack,
Touches and tests, and listens to the wheels.
Guard sounds a warning whistle, points to the clock
With brandished flag, and on his folded flock
Claps the last door: the monster grunts: 'Enough!'
Tightening his load of links with pant and puff.
Under the arch, then forth into blue day,
Glide the processional windows on their way,
And glimpse the stately folk who sit at ease
To view the world like kings taking the seas
In prosperous weather: drifting banners tell
Their progress to the counties; with them goes
The clamour of their journeying; while those
Who sped them stand to wave a last farewell.

SIEGFRIED SASSOON *(1886–1967)*

Fellow-Travelling

Would they, press them, stand against injustice,
Sitting full of yawns in the early morning
Going to London in the marvellous light?
The sun gilds grass, hills
And our inadequate postures;
The laundered landscape folds along the line;
We sip and chew – *they* do,
Reading of wrongs, expecting rights . . .

Half seen beside me, a possible Arab shifts;
Across the table an obvious young businessman
Fixed on *Playboy*, the image of the times –
My summary conviction: nothing there.

The inspector comes swinging from joke to joke,
Again in character, cheering and smart.
The man (Egyptian) on my right
Needs to retain his ticket for expenses.
The collector gestures out to Yorkshire:
Give him the ticket and write for a receipt.
The Egyptian, aimed through Heathrow out of Cairo,
Is badly shaken by the paperwork,
Surely a note or something of the sort . . .

The inspector crosses Jordan and expletes,
Enormous fists pounding near my notebook . . .
A wog to take him on! but doesn't *quite* say so.
Egyptian politeness stumbling on confused . . .
I waveringly suggest
What if he were to sign the seat reservation?
And get the hatchet look reserved for traitors.

At which Flash Harry rests his mag. Near and far
We have supplanted coffee and news.

                                        'You chuck

The buggers at Kings Cross. His ticket
Makes no odds, officious sod.'

They both ascend.
Names demanded, threat swelling to mirror threat.
Then, flashing anger still, Harry says
To go outside, the carriage end, where we hear
For half a county them loudly locked.

My neighbour
Is a doctor with UNESCO; we chat about the world,
The River Nile, happily mile after mile.

Harry returns, a little red, reading a little
Until we catch his eye. He says:

'I've got shops
In Leeds, Newcastle and now this one in London.
I'm always on this train, don't bother with first class.
There's nine inspectors, O.K. except for him.
Last week he made this trouble for a little lass
With two kids and a pram. They're not too bad
On this line except for him and he's a swine.'

MICHAEL STANDEN *(b. 1937)*

from Making the Connection

But first and last
the focal point of magic was the signal-box
with its sophisticated props – the shining grid
of levers bound with coloured tapes,
the panel of instruments, and bells
mounted in parenthesis in wooden clocks –
a place of reverence where, together
with that master-magician, my grandfather,
I could spend a too-brief hour or two
each day, learning how to work the spells
and handle the levers to let the express go hurtling through.

HOWARD SERGEANT *(1914–87)*

Between the Lines

Already dark, and fog seeping in,
that November afternoon
when I accidentally stepped off the edge
of Platform Nine,
emptying the teapot.

An upright landing –
the pot still in my hand
I felt its smooth glaze, unbroken –
but too deep a drop to climb back.

Blurry lights down the line,
a yellowish window-glow
from our small office building
almost at the station's end,
the St Pancras express arriving
on Platform Five. There'd be goods wagons
soon, along this track . . .
I shouted louder.

'Where are you?'
'What are you doing down there?'
Mr Wilkinson's voice . . .
(digging for coal – picking bluebells . . .)
I cried 'Take the teapot',
then held up my arms for the pull.

I owed him a lot – not just this –
but the books he lent me, the talk –
of the Civil War in Spain –
(the 'Reds' weren't the rebels, he said,
as I'd thought from reading Dad's paper,
and Hitler must be stopped – now.)

The others treated me just like a kid
out of school – which I was,
the only female in that smoky den.
Mr Fox said 'Live for today' –

and 'It'll be all the same
a hundred years from now.'
Mr Trigg had been in the Black-and-Tans,
'sorting out the Irish'.
Mr Wilkinson told me he needn't
be proud of that.

I might have known
who'd be the one to hear me shouting,
come to my rescue – pull me up.

LYN COOPER (b.1920)

Signalman

Does he ever envy himself, regret
that he cannot conduct his own life
as he directs others'; as he off-sets
a locomotive to some siding
could he not do the same with his wife
and thus avert her endless chiding;

likewise with his children (who, perhaps,
might be paralleled to a Liverpool special for
both are easily prone to mishaps,
which the neighbours and railway officials each deplore);

and as he would lever a diesel to its shed
to leave it overnight
could he not manacle his devils to their beds –
out of mind, out of sight.

BARTHOLOMEW QUINN (b. 1949)

Taking her Work Home

The management would like to apologise
That the meal which should have arrived
At half-past six has, due to staff
Shortages, been unavoidably delayed.

This is a security announcement:
Will the daughter who left
A plastic carrier bag
In the middle of the stairs

Please remove it at once.
Failure to do so will mean
It will be blown up by a robot.
Unattended luggage is a hazard.

If Bob Reid is on the premises
– Sir Bob Reid –
Will he please come to the kitchen
Where he is urgently needed.

The moon, which is now full,
Shining through the window,
Will call at Melbourne, Liverpool,
Paris, Geneva, Montreal, Moscow

And anywhere anyone might want to go.
Owing to the wrong sort of passenger
We have to announce the cancellation
Of all future services from tomorrow.

PEGGY POOLE *(b. 1925)*

FIVE

The Permanent Way

TRACKS, CUTTINGS AND SIDINGS

The Cuttings

On all my rail journeys out from Lime Street
I've never missed the cuttings
never failed to be excited
by the dark high walls
the blackened sandstone
bedrock of the city, cut into
blasted, shaped by nineteenth century
enterprise. Steam, diesel, electric:
countless trains have slipped out
through these tall passes,
with human freight
each to an individual fate.

And mine: child pleasures first
bound for the London adventure,
secure in parents and a sense of history.
Later, the sad leavetakings,
aware now of personal destiny
the inevitable passage of each of us alone
out through a dark gorge.

GLADYS MARY COLES *(b. 1942)*

After a Romantic Day

The railway bore him through
An earthen cutting out from a city:
There was no scope for view,
Though the frail light shed by a slim young moon
Fell like a friendly tune.

Fell like a liquid ditty,
And the blank lack of any charm
Of landscape did no harm.
The bald steep cutting, rigid, rough,
And moon-lit, was enough
For poetry of place: its weathered face
Formed a convenient sheet whereon
The visions of his mind were drawn.

THOMAS HARDY *(1840–1928)*

The Railway Junction

From here through tunnelled gloom the track
Forks into two; and one of these
Wheels onward into darkening hills,
And one toward distant seas.

How still it is; the signal light
At set of sun shines palely green;
A thrush sings; other sound there's none,
Nor traveller to be seen –

Where late there was a throng. And now,
In peace awhile, I sit alone;
Though soon, at the appointed hour,
I shall myself be gone.

But not their way: the bow-legged groom,
The parson in black, the widow and son,
The sailor with his cage, the gaunt
Gamekeeper with his gun,

That fair one, too, discreetly veiled –
All, who so mutely came, and went,
Will reach those far nocturnal hills,
Or shores, ere night is spent.

I nothing know why thus we met –
Their thoughts, their longings, hopes, their fate:
And what shall I remember, except –
That evening growing late –

That here through tunnelled gloom the track
Forks into two; of these
One into darkening hills leads on,
And one toward distant seas?

WALTER DE LA MARE *(1873–1956)*

A Departure from Solidity

Railroad tracks were different
When I was young.
I used to like
To balance myself on them.
When I couldn't do that,
I stood back and watched
The trains go by.
I never knew where they were going.
Today I find that I know
Too much about destinations.
All the things
Pointing towards the future
Seem to have an end;
And the infinity
I thought I once played on
Was a childhood
I had to walk away from.
I remember now
The time I had to leave
The iron tightrope behind.

TIMOTHY HODOR *(b. 1955)*

The Railway Children

When we climbed the slopes of the cutting
We were eye-level with the white cup
Of the telegraph poles and the sizzling wires.

Like lovely freehand they curved for miles
East and miles west beyond us, sagging
Under their burden of swallows.

We were small and thought we knew nothing
Worth knowing. We thought words travelled the wires
In the shiny pouches of raindrops,

Each one seeded full with the light
Of the sky, the gleam of the lines, and ourselves
So infinitesimally scaled

We could stream through the eye of a needle.

SEAMUS HEANEY *(b. 1939)*

Somewhere North of Wolverhampton

Our train slows in an ambush of asphalt,
blackened brick, rusted rails, cranes thrusting
declamatory fingers into a yellow sky.

We crawl past oases of greenery,
their few trees and shrubs certainly mined
to blow to kingdom come those who might set foot on them.

What lies in wait in those demolished sheds?
Who is it who signals with flashes
of sunlight on factory glass and warehouse window?

And what message? This truck in its siding,
camouflaged with rosebay willowherb,
is booby-trapped to explode in one's face at a touch.

Boys with rods and nets on the canal bank,
intended to look like simple anglers,
are urban guerillas bristling with kalashnikovs.

A vision swells from this concrete rubble:
Society slides into ruin
and we know that nothing to hand is to be trusted.

Neck hairs rise. To stop now would be our end.
We gain speed, pass to less hostile country –
sunburnt scalps of shorn hayfield, cow parsley.
Our fixed smiles pretend nothing has happened.

JOHN WARD *(b. 1915)*

Railway Allotments

Near blackened alcoves
just where the sun's cut off
and peers through grilles
at fantasies of sooted brick
(English bond meticulously ordered),
clear of the frassy tunnels
where diesels bore and cough
and the electric engines sigh,
outside Birmingham Exeter Sheffield Stoke
retired men nurtured
upon implacable texts gingerly unbend
above their linear gardens bordered
with creosoted sleepers,
and shrug their coats and stand
watching for the express to saunter through.

Then turning to their loves,
their strips of peas crosshatched,
Maris Piper stitched in knots of green
along the steady rows, they contemplate
their manuscripts of common prayer
made brilliant with shallots; intercede
that Autumn King and Greyhound may mature,
each white Musselburgh
stand in its paper collar
like a marble pillar, ruby red Detroit
grow thick and firm,
the Stuttgart Giants raised from seed
be slender in the neck and touched
with gold, while the three twenty runs to time
each leisured afternoon.

M.R. PEACOCKE *(b. 1930)*

Past the City Cemetery

Buried by the railway where
     every twenty minutes,
     every ten in rush-hour,
trains vibrate the soil.

'Enough to raise the dead
     living by the railway,'
     you say looking out
from the train window.

     Perhaps!

Maybe the trains compact soil.
     All those coffins
     husband, wife,
covering each other

share the grave-bed.

They loved and bred
     probably hated together.
     Stillborn babies –
never grew to disappoint –

the only truly loved ones?
     Railing spears blur
     as we rattle by
to work, vibrating soil

beneath the rail-bed.
     The subject raised
     the dead crowd with us
into Liverpool Street.

MARGUERITE WOOD *(b. 1923)*

The Railway Carriage Couple

Our home's a railway carriage
And it cannot be denied
That you might describe our dwelling
As a little bit on the side
Yet it has the odd advantages
Where other housing fails
And we're on the straight and narrow
So we can't go off the rails!

Our decor is original
It's simple but it's good
With little plaques screwed on the wall
That give the type of wood
And up above the headrest
Of the seat marked number five
Is a photograph of Cheddar Gorge
In case we don't arrive.

Yes we're the railway carriage couple
With the long drive at the front
Or it might be at the back
If we feel like a change, and shunt.
We're a little isolated
But if ever I get bored
And feel like communicating
I stand up and pull the cord.

I don't do much entertaining,
It's too cramped, you see, by far
For dining graciously
Because it's not a buffet car,
So we eat out in the corridor,
My husband doesn't care
But I like to face the engine
Even though it isn't there.

Of course there is a certain problem
Which we have and always will
In that we cannot use the toilet
While the train is standing still
So we built one just beside us
And we glazed it in with glass
The first time my husband used it
He came back and said 'First Class!'

We have a little garden
We don't buy much in the town
You can see us any evening
Raking clinker up and down
You might see us in our door
If you don't travel by too fast
And we'll let down two holes in the leather strap
And wave as you go past.

PAM AYRES *(b. 1947)*

Penwortham Railway Bankings

The spreading May bush more than half conceals
a red eviscerated mattress.
Grey asphalt, like a tortoise nestles into
a snug bed of dandelions.
Down dark mysterious slopes,
frail bluebells boldly challenge
the rule of scrap iron and disembowelled settees.
Grey rain-soaked newspapers
flash their dead headlines
through tufts of buttercups.
Ruins such as Greece and Italy never knew –
an old Scout hut no longer valued
obscenely exposes its vitals.
Vandals hold their secret parties here,
against a decor of graffiti,
leaving cracked mugs and scorched black grass.

In Maytime, nature overflows with life
to compensate despoilers' dreary work.
But come December, just to walk these banks
is to despair at endless human persecution
of nature's beauty, constantly renewed.

HOPE BUNTON *(b. 1921)*

Hobo Sapiens

(With acknowledgements to John Masefield)

I must go down to the tracks again
And move on to another town,
For bumming around in this old place
Is starting to get me down,
And look around for a big box car
I can climb aboard unseen,
For a quiet sleep through the summer night
As we rumble over the plain.

I must go down to the tracks again
And look out for an hour or two's work, –
Painting a fence or sweeping a yard
For some patronising jerk.
And a Mission House on an empty street
That's there at the end of the day,
With a cup of soup and a wooden bunk
To keep the cold away.

I must go down to the tracks again,
For the past is a running sore
And I have to keep moving ahead of it
Till I can run no more.
And all I ask is oblivion
From a slug of some cheap red wine,
As I sprawl here on a jolting floor
And wait for the end of the line.

JOHN TICKNER *(b. 1940)*

the railway inn

the railway's gone
that used to bring me here
years without fail
pushed one way, pulled the other,
along the single line from Tillynaught;

between the steep brae
and the rusting green gasholder
boys race motorbikes
across the scuffed scrub where the station
stood, and only boats of shallow draught

lie in the harbour
between the banks of silt.
from the north seas
the weather's closing in, clouds thick
as stonewalls, rain thin as my thoughts;

another glen grant and an o.v.d.
with ginger, please, sandy.

DAVE CALDER *(b. 1946)*

Abandoned Cutting

A green wound closes
Where rails lately rusted
and pulleyed wires pulled
distant signals to attention.
Cowslips lord over grass,
heads bowed like lanky girls.
Hazel and dog rose briar
take bolt and fishplate
hostage or treasure
colonising old ways
no longer permanent.
It was exciting once:
here lone travellers
at rest between stops
had time to stare outside
and see for the first time
clots of wild strawberries
pricking green blood red.
Easy to forget days and diagrams
fired, peppered and steamed
by moving mists of Welsh coal.
A place like no other,
always on the way somewhere,
a deep gash for passing
between a far off to or from.
Hard now to recall the movement
of anything beyond a season,
remember connections kept,
the distances joined
or people who once passed here.
Now usefulness is done
growing takes over
and cuttings we gazed at
there and all the way home, change,
healing into forgotten nowheres.

PAUL BERRY *(b. 1953)*

The Galloway Line

And it shall be as this:
the faint trace of a main line
through the whaup cry places;
marigolds grow wild on platforms,
water troughs and broken signals.

Round these surfaces the rising forestry.
The dykes erected when the black beasts came,
the dykes the growers failed to level
crumble under weather
and are left.
Breaking dyke from breaking croft
from breaking Roman wall.

The distant Solway, a withdrawing sea,
leaves Wigtown with a harbour on a hill,
while always on the cattle way
to Ireland lorries snake;
our purpose flows.

And those who travelled
on these scrag lines slightly hear
a tightening of grass
a late steam whistle
in the rain cloud's corner.

ROBIN MUNRO *(b. 1946)*

Exchange Station

My feet echo in this open ended grave,
I walk along the platform,
Saving my thoughts
For remembered times.
When – leaving Mum and Dad –
I ran to see the engine,
That hissed quietly
Like a sleeping dragon.

Wheels towered above me,
Oily men with oily rags
Polished shining brass, unnecessarily.

Later,
Sitting in the carriage on moquette seats,
Looking at pictures of Skegness and Scarborough,
We were pulled to Ainsdale.

In the sea, sun and burning sand,
We bathed, burned and buried treasures
We never found again.
Treasures we still are looking for.

Then back on the train with shells and stones
Red shoulders, sandy toes,
Back to Exchange Station.

I would exchange for that,
This station,
From which they've ripped the track,
Made matchwood of the office,
And boarded up the hatch,
So that Second class citizens
Such as you and me
From here no longer travel
Except in memory.

ROY POWELL

Privacy

Through the window of the paused train
I saw that the station's public lavatory
for men had been demolished, its rubble
cleared away and all that was left
was the original floor of russet tile.
It, and the levelled walls, were flush
with the platform that surrounded it
on four sides, like a wide picture frame.
Around the row of six holes, where
the shiny white toilet bowls had once
stood, the tiles were worn smooth
and stained with a patina of green
unlike those around the sink holes
which were sharp-edged and clean.
I noticed the waiting passengers,
women especially, milling around this
lifesize floorplan, not encroaching
but staring – and I twinged in sympathy
for the former users, their partitioned
space now Berlin-walled; something
previously forbidden unveiled;
like one's soiled handkerchief or
pornographic book being revealed.
It seemed wrong to me that areas
once so private – for defecation,
micturation and ejaculation – were now
so publicly exposed. Somehow, even the
ghosts of those sitters, standers and
kneelers had a right to some privacy, too.

ANDREW PYE *(b. 1963)*

Too Late

The mystery of what happens
has wrapped this station in a shroud
and splinters from its vandalised glass doors
have torn the membranes of old dreams
to make it one with parting.

My future is so short,
so like a Winter's day
before the blinds are drawn.
Only the homespun past is long,
stretching behind me
like a length of cloth
far down the road
where people that I know
as well as my own hand
live out their lives
behind the stock brick walls
and there is no time left
to walk away
and catch the train
to a different place.

DEIRDRE ARMES-SMITH *(b. 1922)*

Grand Central Railway

That distant rush of engines: is it
locomotives, furnace
roaring still as the strewn components rust?
Or cars and lorries on the motorway
racing between cities, making 90?

Winter swings in here on the iron hinge
of frost; wind shudders
saplings into a sound-wraith
of pluming steam. They catch
the slanted gold of dwindling afternoon –

grey ash-silk, hawthorn tangle
serene on quiet banks that shut
the estate out. I walk on tarry asphalt
that frays at edges into fresh-chipped stone
merging with work-soiled ballast from the Line

that bedded polished rails. Long-rotted stumps
of signals lie in weeds and have forgotten
their semaphore authority;
an ancient swab's preserved in oil – dropped
by a railwayman whose pulses beat with steam

pistons. Now, where tappers brewed their tea
old men throw slobbered balls for dogs who rush
inventing urgencies; and overhead
above a glow that leaves this walk in shadow
a growling jet plane arrows towards the sun.

MARGARET TOMS (b. 1928)

Branch Line

And coming back, wind-ruffled and grubby
After a tramping weekend, she dumped
Tumbling on the kitchen table great rusty bolts,
And grimed cubed nuts, and talked of the track
The railway abandoned twenty years ago.

And thin delicate rounded pebbles, alabaster,
Polished flint and granite, soft shining
Like thumb nails. And I could see her on that beach,
By that incoming tide, levels of time like layered slate.

And seeing her more and more distanced as she walks away,
On up the branch line, between the uncut hedges,
Beneath the cutting and the disused dripping bridges

I watch my daughter branching out; geologist, historian
Leaving on the table with the coffee cups, a frayed map
And the building stones, the nuts and bolts of life.

DAVID PALMER *(b. 1935)*

Terminus

The journey ends
at a shut-down station
on the wrong line;
light fading
over unfamiliar fields;
no train back.

One hears distant hammers:
a gang is demolishing the track.

JOHN WARD *(b. 1915)*

SIX

Off the Rails

DELAYS, DRAMAS AND DISASTERS

Hold-up

I'm sorry, but I just can't tolerate
British Rail excuses when schedules slump,
shilly-shallying the one thing I hate.

And now we're in for a more prolonged wait –
some *nut* on the bridge threatening to jump!
I'm sorry, but I just can't tolerate

cops' half-baked forays to coax and placate
with no thought for *us* marooned in this dump,
shillyshallying. The one thing I hate

is a Force without spine: a postwar trait.
Ex-para myself I'm used to booting rump.
I'm sorry, but I just can't tolerate

all this pussyfooting. A half-hour late –
and high time *I* cracked the whip on that chump
shillyshallying. (The one thing *I* hate!)

So I pushed him, m'lud. Didn't hesitate.
A short enough drop, and yes, quite a thump.
I'm sorry. But I can't tolerate
shillyshallying – the one thing I *hate*.

SYLVIA TURNER (b. 1933)

Complaint to British Rail

An engine banging in the night
woke two sleepers side by side
caused a coupling of their thighs
and shunted forth another life!

TREVOR KNEALE (b. 1934)

Going Nowhere

Locked in a train –
train going nowhere, fixed beside
oblivion. It is
warm here, there are lights,
the comfort makes a womb of it.
Outside
splatters of rain
mottle the greasy dark
refracting
hazy haloes around a streetlight
into diffusion. Twigs
pierce the blackness of grass and sky.
Inside
cigarettes breathe air into staleness
coursing through too many.
The glass
is crusted with rust, ageing our wait.
Heat buffets our legs. The cold
of being among alien others
suffocates.
Locked in a train, and up and down the line
on station platforms husbands,
children, lovers all go home,
shaking their heads.
We are a million miles from Adlestrop –
and just this side of hell.

ALISON CHISHOLM *(b. 1952)*

Station Scene

'The two-fifteen is running late
and will arrive at three'
chants the announcer
tonelessly.

Thick railway teacups
gathering grime,
watery dishwash
for threepence a time
but the whisky at two-and-six
is sublime.

Worried bowler-hatted men
on business bent,
war or no war,
cost plus ten-per-cent.
If there were no profits,
how could we pay the rent?

Khaki splashes all over the platform,
kit piled high,
sergeant-pilots brown of face,
keen of eye,
and a curly-headed sailor
kissing his girl goodbye.

'The two-fifteen is running late
and will arrive at three'
repeats the announcer
monotonously.

LYN COOPER *(b. 1920)*

Delays and Departures

(For Joanna)

At Exeter Central, waiting to connect,
I limbo through an hour or so
Of cancelled time, and recollect
How I met you here six years ago.
Then, as now, the train long gone
An arterial line neatly cut
We watched as others rivered on
Blanking out as the air slammed shut.

Swerving towards home some sense of source
That lay beyond the hot, thin fields
The expresses kept their steady course
Towards wives and kids and evening meals
In houses bright with birthday cakes.
Now, six years on, I watch the same
Trains slow like hearts and brake
And breathe their fastnesses again.

Then embark alone and half-afraid,
Knowing happiness and quiet cancers chance
Through all life's network of delays
Regardless of the circumstance.
Six years ago, I stayed, you left;
Disconnection, half-undone,
Daily stepping through our deaths,
Still dimly aware of somewhere's sun.

MARTYN J. LOWERY *(b. 1961)*

Delay

The people in the train
too many, too close.
I should walk home over hills,
by the river, the sea
      or past a slagheap where children play –
no respite: the doors fly open,
command. We have no choice
we enter and sit. We move,
choice suffocates. Each wall sells,
spends our wage.
We take on speed
      the disregarded feat
the last century's bricks
show through the window.
We either sit and stare or read:
habits abound. Mine's incurable,
I look around me
      – perhaps I'm shortsighted.
We must hurry, know where we're going
newspapers point the black path home
to television and tea. A man rises,
lifts the black habit that has clung to his hand all day

      the train stops
        not there yet.

A calm comes upon us
– a slight delay.
In the corner, a final rustle
the brains of a businessman
fall into his paper and are folded away.

A minute goes by. Dust settles.
A secret society.
Londoners
we sit in silence, like ghosts
still capable of the word 'love'
it circles now,
        it presses most.

CHRIS BENDON (b. 1950)

Between Stations

Between stations
not anywhere in particular
you put your neck on the line;
the train was delayed
above the water-meadows;
an ordinary suicide said the guard.

For a moment no one spoke.
Looking out,
I walked the weir-gate after snow;
saw the young swans
dip to the meltwater
below the roar of the foam.

And I have remembered
the marvellous interlacing
of their throats
against an unspilled reach
not anywhere in particular
but between stations.

PAULINE STAINER (b. 1941)

from The Tay Bridge Disaster

Beautiful Railway Bridge of the Silv'ry Tay!
Alas! I am very sorry to say
That ninety lives have been taken away
On the last Sabbath day of 1879,
Which will be remember'd for a very long time.

'Twas about seven o'clock at night,
And the wind it blew with all its might,
And the rain came pouring down,
And the dark clouds seem'd to frown,
And the Demon of the air seem'd to say –
'I'll blow down the Bridge of Tay.'

When the train left Edinburgh
The passengers' hearts were light and felt no sorrow,
But Boreas blew a terrific gale,
Which made their hearts for to quail,
And many of the passengers with fear did say –
'I hope God will send us safe across the Bridge of Tay.'

So the train sped on with all its might,
And Bonnie Dundee soon hove in sight,
And the passengers' hearts felt light,
Thinking they would enjoy themselves on the New Year,
With their friends at home they lov'd most dear,
And wish them all a happy New Year.

So the train mov'd slowly along the Bridge of Tay,
Until it was about midway,
Then the central girders with a crash gave way,
And down went the train and passengers into the Tay!
The Storm Fiend did loudly bray,
Because ninety lives had been taken away,
On the last Sabbath day of 1879
Which will be remember'd for a very long time . . .

WILLIAM McGONAGALL *(1830–1902)*

White Trains Log

MARCH. Woke
shaking from dreams
lay for a long time
while the train
grumbled away
through town.

APRIL. They
come hourly
through darkness
concealing
black suns radiant
on yellow skies.

JUNE. Night
too short and
threadbare now
to hide
the poisoned cups
they send.

SEPTEMBER. More
often than hours
the trembling
down deep
hugging myself
for comfort.

OCTOBER. Woke
to silence
five nights
and no trains
this, this
worst of all.

ROBERT DRAKE *(b. 1955)*

Inter-city

The train was worse than any tin
of sardines, which at least keep still.
I rolled, a misdirected ball, along
a corridor that seemed to stretch
from Euston beyond Watford
encumbered by suitcases, a typewriter,
and a bewildered dog, until at last
I found one vacant seat.

Slumped, exhausted, sweat pouring
down my back, I watched rain slash
windows (jerky drops chased upwards
by speed and down by natural law.)
wetness seeped into my brain
prompting the realisation that
I had left the bath-tap running
in my empty flat.

The non-stop journey became a two hour
drowning; the woman opposite slurped
coffee, beside me a man's nose kept
dripping, a newspaper featured an article
on underwater sports, the countryside
excelled in ponds, canals and streams.

My mind sank beneath cascades
of details – floating clothes and carpets –
and, in the flat below, sodden
ceilings. The Yale key in my pocket
torpedoed any hope.

PEGGY POOLE *(b. 1925)*

Lines

Hot summer sizzled axles
June, July; August's approach
gave metal wheel a flat tyre.
Three anti-bandit coaches were unlined,
coincidence's curse.

A florin moon lit Bridgego Bridge,
silvered parallel tracks
above damp grass, loose rock.
Two forty . . . fifty . . . three . . .
watch hands steeled their path, cigar starred.

The bulk of black throbbed rails,
obeyed Sears Crossing's sign.
Clank of uncoupling receded
as urge to get a vacuum
sucked in the blooded innocent.

And then high-value carriages were swarmed,
axe smashed, assaulted.
Invaders hurtled through the windows,
eased doors until their space
let bags spew down the grass.

Sacks passed from hand to hand
linked a chain of avarice, unbroken
until one made safe the victims,
proffered cigarettes. Last load
was left, time compromised.

Today the lines bask
glinting morning, pewter night.
Only listen when a train rumbles,
bucks the route through Cheddington,
for whispers whose audacity still shocks.

ALISON CHISHOLM *(b. 1952)*

Sleeper

Dear Steward, we're sorry we shock you like this
but you were so kind when we got on at Euston
– not everyone can cope with illness.
You'll find my husband's briefcase on
the rack near the window. The key's in
a blue envelope in my make-up case
(the zipped compartment). I think that's everything.
I suppose you think it's odd to go like this
but our neighbours are foreign, our only daughter
has small children, a husband who's less
than useful. Please destroy this note before
we arrive. The police will deal with the rest.
The enclosed is for your trouble. As we both come
from Edinburgh, it seems like going home.

PATRICIA POGSON *(b. 1944)*

Impatience

The train was late; then did not come at all.
People on the platform crowded about,
Outstared the clock in intense idleness
Or looked along the line. Another time
It would have been unseen, what caught the hem
Of our attention: the dusty city mouse
We saw tick-tack across the track, and fret
As if with our impatience – making it small.

PETER WALTON (b. 1936)

Note on the Troubles

From middle class civilities,
the neat suburban properties,
they came to board the roaring train,
to bucket to the clamorous town.
Entombed in newspapers, they read
through green, oblivious countryside
of international bickerings,
the play of personalities,
the sports page and the comic strips
and Ulster's casual murderings;
while, overlooked, a neat valise
ticks closer to apocalypse.

DAVID HOLLIDAY (b. 1931)

The Schonau Express

Nine hours of boredom in the darkness.
Humming the only shabbat song we know
as the crippled express rocks us into Austria.
In the thick fog of our carriage, shabby families doze.
The children fight and scuffle down crowded
corridors, or listen to the bristles sprouting on
their fathers' chins.

Norma's dream is a blurred travelogue
of tattered maps and orange groves;
summer igniting the singing globes of fruit.
We travel lighter than the rest, rolling to the
monotonous pant of steam as the engine strains
towards Bernau.
I stretch out wet fingers to touch her lips;
blood has caked on this steamy pane, brown
against the blinding glare of frost.

I ask one guard our time of arrival.
He looks up from his grimy clockface of playing cards
to stamp 'Who needs to know?' on the back of my wrist.
In all the confusion we've forgotten the name
of our destination.
Norma still sleeps under my grey trenchcoat,
her skirt is melting against her thigh.

VINCENT MORRISON *(b. 1952)*

The Journey

'If it were not so we would have told you.'
That night on the crowded train they played cards
remembering Sion always between stations.

The children peed among them till the dawn
when sleepily they woke to see the houses
and the kind human helmets among stones.

Gently the train steamed as if exhausted.
The soul remembers Sion washed and clean,
deloused, unenvious, waiting nakedly.

'If it were not so we would have told you.'
The hiss belonged to legend, where began
the toil that sent us out with the heavy spade.

IAIN CRICHTON SMITH *(b. 1928)*

Unchecked

Course, us regulars understood
that brake pipes should be painted red
and what that meant for a full tank train.
But we knew nothing was as it seemed.

We'd go along and test each one
(red or white was all the same)
so we could check if red spoke true,
(for colours often were mixed up)
see what brake force tons we had,
see how fast the train could run.
You couldn't go with no brakes on –
needed a brake van on the back.

Came a day when the guard was new
and the regular driver was off sick.
Seeing all pipes painted red
the stand-ins thought they'd full brake force
but neither of them were regulars, see?

Two yellow signals were passed at speed,
the driver braked but his train sped on;
at the next yellow he tried again
still it didn't slow at all.
Now they were fast approaching red.
They raced past red and then found out
their emergency brakes had no effect!
Ahead at the junction they could see
a freight liner from the other road.
A hell of a lot of damage was done
as the last five wagons of the freight
were hit by the runaway brakeless train.

Knowing the danger they were in
(a four hundred foot fall not far off)
the driver said 'I'll see you up there!'
'What d'you mean? Can't we jump?'

'Where can we jump to? There's no sense.'

No one knew why the train pulled up
feet away from that perilous drop
(you can see it still on the way to Crewe).
Both survived, but were broken men
and all because they did not know
that trucks with each pipe painted red
might not in fact have any brakes.

Course, us regulars would have known
for we knew nothing was as it seemed.

PEGGY POOLE *(b. 1925)*

The Journey

I don't remember much about that time
Not even my own age. I guess when asked.
No family snapshots remain. The lime
Saw to that. My parents' faces, masked
By layer after layer of lost years
Become unclearer as I leave their age
Behind. I grew old. They did not. Arrears
Of debt accumulate in love and rage.
The carriage had no windows. From a crack
I looked at fields accelerating fast
Through Summer with wheat as high as a cow's back
Recoiling from the train as it rushed past.
We jolted over points. I ate my rations
As we careered through peaceful Polish stations.

ANTHONY KNIGHT *(b. 1951)*

No Return

Death camps, fifty years on

Your candles flicker on the railway track
that led to hell, the camps of hair and bone.
We are their ghosts, O do not call us back.

They tied the human spirit in a sack
of ash and smoke, these little flames atone:
your candles flicker on the railway track.

They had their killing place, a shower, a shack.
Our people stood together and alone.
We are their ghosts, O do not call us back.

For who can free tormentors from their rack,
tormented from their pain? By faith alone
your candles flicker on the railway track.

We stood behind the wire and watched them stack
our people into piles of earth and stone.
We are their ghosts, O do not call us back.

This station of the cross is draped in black.
Against our griefs the winter winds have blown.
Your candles flicker on the railway track.
We are their ghosts, O do not call us back.

SUSAN SKINNER *(b. 1935)*

Storm Damage

She was never the same,
anyone could have found him,
it happened to be her.

He was late, you see;
three times she'd boiled the kettle,
hung breakfast bacon before the fire;

she took the lantern
the thick black shawl.
The lamp in the window
reached to the end of the lane.

It wasn't much of a job
two trains
night and morning;
three miles to the station
half an hour by bike.

He'd set off at five,
man the crossing,
see the goods through,
ride home, still in the dark.

It was the Elm
across the road.

She was never the same;
that look in her eyes
the silence –

                DORA KENNEDY *(b. 1911)*

The End of the Line

When the old man
was at last posted to the Underground
just before I reached my eighth birthday
it was difficult to convince
me that he was not still somewhere around
opening level-crossing gates and manipulating
levers to let some ghostly Pullman
with a shower of sparks go scorching through,
or that he would not suddenly spring into view
in a subterranean gust of smoke.
His departure made such little sense.
It was, rather, an obscene if terminal joke.
For I lost, without recourse,
not only my grandfather and a discriminating
friend, but also my public, my platform, my source
of income, and the magic of the railway,
at a single stroke.

I've been travelling without a valid ticket ever since.

HOWARD SERGEANT   *(1914–87)*

NOTES TO THE POEMS

16   **Liverpool Overhead Railway in the Thirties**   This railway opened in 1893 and was closed down in 1956. A ginnel (*not* a misprint for 'gunnel') is a narrow alley or path between high walls or buildings.

21   **585**   Emily Dickinson's poems are not always printed in the form used here, and some have been given titles – I have seen this one with the title 'Locomotive'. However, for me her frequent use of dashes is more authentic. Her poems in Faber's *The Complete Emily Dickinson* are set out in numerical order – hence '585'

24   **Night Mail**   According to Edward Mendelson, who edited *W.H. Auden: Collected Poems* in 1976, this was written in July 1935. It was used in *Night Mail*, a film made by the General Post Office Film Unit in 1936.

26   **Closely Observed Films**   This is a commissioned poem. Film directors have frequently tuned into the romance of trains, and Martyn Halsall manages to include references to, among others, *Brief Encounter*, *The Bridge on the River Kwai* and *Doctor Zhivago*.

28   **Tank Engines Rule – O.K?**   Generations of children have counted Thomas the Tank Engine as their friend, and I commissioned Hilary Tinsley to make sure that he took his place among his larger brethren.

28   **My Train Set**   This was submitted among hundreds of other poems for the hour-long celebration of poetry by young people on BBC Radio Merseyside. Timothy, who was nine years old when he wrote this poem, read it on air himself.

33   **Not Adlestrop**   Many poems have been inspired by Edward Thomas's Adlestrop (see page 32), perhaps the most favourite of all railway poems; none can match this.

35   **Suspense at Preston**   Jean Sergeant's poem picks up the fear that was felt in the days before trains had buffet cars when a travelling companion ran for a cup of tea if the train stopped at a station. Would he or she come back in time before the train moved on?

36   **Returning Home**   The poet has created a delightful link between lost luggage, albeit a plastic bag, the characters who make up platform crowds and the giants who live on in our minds.

37 **Gare du Midi**   This was written in December 1938, according to Edward Mendelson (see the note to 'Night Mail', page 24, above).

42 **Station Buffet**   Yes, it is all but a song, but poems and songs *can* be interchangeable . . .

43 **Waiting to be Met**   A painful memory festered in the poet's mind until it was released in 1995 by the writing of this poem. It may reflect the experience of other evacuees.

45 **The Wayside Station**   Edwin Muir wrote this poem in the winter of 1940–41, when he was living in St Andrews and travelling every day to Dundee, where he worked in the Food Office.

46 **Jubilate – Railway Imperial**   Between 1983 and 1993 Windsor and Eton Central Station was the venue for the Royalty and Empire Exhibition, which was about the Diamond Jubilee of Queen Victoria.

72 **The Guard's Van**   Like 'Broadening the Mind' (see page 110), this poem was submitted to BBC North for *Write Now* (the weekly half-hour programme of stories and poetry) only weeks after I had begun to compile this anthology. A clear case of serendipity!

79 **Girl in a Train**   Until I came to put this anthology together I had no idea how many passengers conducted affairs – if only in their heads – with a girl on a train.

98 **Travelling**   Returning home from Cornwall in March 1995, I discovered this poem in the brochure produced by the Looe Valley Line Working Party. I understand that it has long been used in verse-speaking classes.

106 **First Train to Devil's Bridge**   The poet says that this is, as far as she knows, the only narrow-gauge railway that was part of British Rail. It runs between Aberystwyth and Devil's Bridge.

121 **To the Late Thomas Sharp**   Chairman Mr Mellor, who gave this tribute at a meeting in 1847, was 'a private workman in the concern in the Department of the Erectors. He enjoyed the distinguished honour of having been selected by his fellow workmen to fill that high post', Thomas Sharp, born in 1780, started a workshop in 1806. In 1833, joined by his brothers, the firm, which later became the Atlas works, built their first locomotive, *Experiment*. I am indebted to Michael Sharp, Thomas Sharp's great-great-nephew, for both this information and for the verse tribute.

122 **The Spiritual Railway**   When pouring through every book on railways I could find – reference, prose and poetry – I came across this rare salute to the men who 'worked their guts out' and 'took appalling risks on the job to save a few minutes, and who died in large numbers of accident and disease'. Christopher Somerville (*Working Old Railways*, David & Charles, 1979) writes movingly

about the navvies who built the railways, and he also lists some of their unusual names: 'Dolly-legged Punch, Shadow and Bones, Starch-'em-Stiff and Scandalous.'

ACKNOWLEDGEMENTS

The editor and publishers have made every effort to contact copyright holders whose work is included in this book; however, omissions may inadvertently have occurred, and they will be pleased to hear from any copyright holder whose work is not properly acknowledged below.

Dannie Abse: 'Not Adlestrop' and 'After a Departure' from *Selected Poems*, © Dannie Abse. Reprinted by permission of Sheil Land Associates and the author.

Deirdre Armes-Smith: 'Too Late' from *Untold Care*, 1991, © Deirdre Armes-Smith. Reprinted by permission of the National Poetry Foundation and the author.

W.H. Auden: 'Night Mail' and 'Gare du Midi' from *Collected Poems*, © W.H. Auden. Reprinted by permission of Faber and Faber.

Pam Ayres: 'The Railway Carriage Couple' from *The Works*, © Pam Ayres. Reprinted by permission of the author.

Barbara Balch: 'Commuter Train' from *After the Storm*, © Barbara Balch. Reprinted by permission of *The Literary Review* and the author.

Wendy Bardsley: 'Holidays: Platform 8', © Wendy Bardsley. Reprinted by permission of the author.

Chris Bendon: 'Delay' from *Outposts*, © Chris Bendon. Reprinted by permission of the author.

Paul Berry: 'Abandoned Cutting' from *Envoi Summer Anthology*, 1989, © Paul Berry. Reprinted by permission of Envoi and the author.

John Betjeman: 'Pershore Station, *or* A Liverish Journey First Class' from *Collected Poems*, 1958, 'The Metropolitan Railway. Baker Street Station Buffet' from *A Few Late Chrysanthemums*, 1954, and 'A Mind's Journey to Diss' from *Collected Poems*, 1958, © John Betjeman. Reprinted by permission of John Murray.

Christine Boothroyd: 'Down and Out, Paddington Station' from *Doors 30*, © Christine Boothroyd. Reprinted by permission of the author.

Mary Brett: 'Deganwy Villanelle' from *Inklings Anthology*, © Mary Brett. Reprinted by permission of the author.

Hope Bunton: 'Penwortham Railway Bankings' from *Until All is Silent*, © Hope Bunton. Reprinted by permission of Envoi Publications and the author.

Dave Calder: 'the railway inn' from *Buchan*, 1983, © Dave Calder. Reprinted by permission of Merseyside Minibooks and the author.

Charles Causley: 'In the Dome Car' from *Collected Poems*, 1988, © Charles Causley. Reprinted by permission of David Higham Associates.

Alison Chisholm: 'Strange Call' and 'Meeting the Empty Train' from *Paperbirds*, reprinted by permission of Stride, 'Going Nowhere' from *Flying Free*, reprinted by permission of Mersey Minibooks, and 'Lines', © Alison Chisholm, reprinted by permission of the author.

Gladys Mary Coles: 'Journey – London to Cambridge' from *Leafburners* and 'The Cuttings' from *Liverpool Folio*, © Gladys Mary Coles. Reprinted by permission of Duckworth and the author.

Lyn Cooper: 'Between the Lines' from *Staple 24* and 'Station Scene' from *More Poems of the Second World War*, © Lyn Cooper. Reprinted by permission of Dent and the author.

Wendy Cope: 'Strugnell's Sonnets' from *Making Cocoa for Kingsley Amis*, © Wendy Cope. Reprinted by permission of Faber and Faber.

Frances Cornford: 'Parting in Wartime' and 'To a Fat Lady Seen from the Train' from *Twentieth Century Women's Poets*, 1987, © Frances Cornford. Reprinted by permission of Faber and Faber.

Doris Corti: 'Waiting to be Met', © Doris Corti. Reprinted by permission of the author.

John Cotton: 'Holiday's End' from *Scenes from a Suburban Childhood*, 1980, © John Cotton. Reprinted by permission of Mandeville Press and the author.

John Critchley: 'The Railway Tramp' from *Iota 27*, © John Critchley. Reprinted by permission of the author.

Beryl Cross: 'Jubilate – Railway Imperial', © Beryl Cross. Reprinted by permission of the author.

Margaret Curwen: 'Railway Song' from *Guildhall Anthology*, 1983, © Margaret Curwen.

Lisbeth David: 'King's Cross to Liverpool' from *The Voice of War*, 1989, © Lisbeth David. Reprinted by permission of Michael Joseph and The Salamander Oasis Trust.

Jonathan Davidson: 'The Train Spotter' from *The Gregory Anthology*, Arc Publications, 1994 © Jonathan Davidson. Reprinted by permission of the author.

Alan Davis: 'Revenant' from *Mocking Bowlers*, 1994, © Alan Davis. Reprinted by permission of the National Poetry Foundation and the author.

Walter de la Mare: 'The Railway Junction' from *Collected Poems*, 1946, © Walter de la Mare. Reprinted by permission of Faber and Faber.

Robert Drake: 'White Trains Log' from *Poet's England: Cumbria*, 1995, © Robert Drake. Reprinted by permission of Headland Publications and the author.

T.S. Eliot: 'Skimbleshanks: The Railway Cat' from *Old Possum's Book of Practical Cats*, © T.S. Eliot. Reprinted by permission of Faber and Faber.

Roger Elkin: 'Train Journey: Eller Fields', © Roger Elkin. Reprinted by permission of the author.

Gerald England: 'Arrival in Nottingham' from *Poet's England: Nottinghamshire*, © Gerald England. Reprinted by permission of Brentham Press and the author.

U.A. Fanthorpe: 'Father in the Railway Buffet' from *Selected Poems*, © U.A. Fanthorpe. Reprinted by permission of Peterloo Poets.

Patricia Frazer: 'Station Buffet' from *Pause 29*, © Patricia Frazer. Reprinted by permission of the National Poetry Foundation and the author.

Robert Frost: 'The Figure in the Doorway' from *The Poetry of Robert Frost*, © Robert Frost. Reprinted by permission of Jonathan Cape.

John Fuller: 'In a Railway Compartment', © John Fuller. Reprinted by permission of the author.

Roy Fuller: 'The End of a Leave' from *More Poems from the Second World War*, © John Fuller. Reprinted by permission of Dent and John Fuller.

Sue Gerrard: 'The Rainhill Trials (October 1829)' from *Poet's England: Lancashire*, © Sue Gerrard. Reprinted by permission of Headland Publications and the author.

David Gill: 'Steam Day at Didcot' from *Staple 26*, © David Gill.

Martyn Halsall: 'Closely Observed Films', © Martyn Halsall. Reprinted by permission of the author.

Thomas Hardy: 'In a Waiting-Room', 'At the Railway Station, Upway', 'On the Departure Platform', 'A Parting-Scene', 'Midnight on the Great Western', 'Faintheart in a Railway Train' and 'After a Romantic Day' from *The Collected Poems of Thomas Hardy*, 1930 (reprinted 1974), © Thomas Hardy. Reprinted by permission of Macmillan.

Frances Harland: 'Communication Cord' from *Envoi 21*, © Frances Harland. Reprinted by permission of Envoi and J.D. Marshall.

Ray Harman: 'The Old Great Western Line' from *A Resounding Voice*, © Ray Harman. Reprinted by permission of Horseshoe and the author.

Timothy Heal: 'My Train Set', © Timothy Heal. Reprinted by permission of BBC Radio Merseyside and the author.

Seamus Heaney: 'Getting on on the Railways' and 'The Railway Children' from *Station Island*, © Seamus Heaney. Reprinted by permission of Faber and Faber.

Diana Hendry: 'Making Connections' from *Peterloo Preview 3*, © Diana Hendry. Reprinted by permission of Peterloo Poets and the author.

Phoebe Hesketh: 'The Leave Train' from *The Leave Train*, © Phoebe Hesketh. Reprinted by permission of Enitharmon Press and the author.

Richard Hill: 'at the station' from *Five Dinners to Cheap Cuts*, 1980, © Richard Hill. Reprinted by permission of the author.

Mary Hodgson: 'Amtrak Return' from *New World*, 1990, © Mary Hodgson. Reprinted by permission of Envoi Publications and the author.

Timothy Hodor: 'A Departure from Solidity' from *Pennine Ink*, © Timothy Hodor. Reprinted by permission of the author.

David Holliday: 'Notes on the Troubles' from *Outposts 110*, 1976, © David Holliday. Reprinted by permission of the author.

Geoffrey Holloway: 'Diesel Driver' from *The Leaping Pool*, © Geoffrey Holloway. Reprinted by permission of the National Poetry Foundation and the author.

Michael Horovitz: 'Intercity Animal' from *Wordsounds and Sightlines: New and Collected Poems*, © Michael Horovitz. Reprinted by permission of Sinclair-Stevenson.

Brian Jones: 'The Spitfire on the Northern Line' from *The Spitfire on the Northern Line*, © Brian Jones. Reprinted by permission of Carcanet.

Sylvia Kantaris: 'Waving Goodbye' from *IPSE*, May 1977, © Sylvia Kantaris. Reprinted by permission of the author.

Jackie Kay: 'Sassenachs' from *Two's Company*, © Jackie Kay. Reprinted by permission of Blackie and the author.

Judith Kazantzis: 'Railroad Station' from *The Rabbit Magician Plate*, © Judith Kazantzis. Reprinted by permission of Sinclair-Stevenson and the author.

Dora Kennedy: 'Storm Damage', © Dora Kennedy. Reprinted by permission of the author.

Cynthia Kitchen: 'Strangers on a Train' from *Lancaster Literature Festival Prizewinners*, 1995, © Cynthia Kitchen. Reprinted by permission of the author.

Trevor Kneale: 'Complaint to British Rail' from *Equinox and other Poems*, 1972, © Trevor Kneale. Reprinted by permission of Rondo Publications and the author.

Anthony Knight: 'The Journey' from *Orbis*, 1995, © Anthony Knight. Reprinted by permission of Orbis and the author.

Lotte Kramer: 'The Loneliness of an Empty Railway Carriage' from *Earthquake and other Poems*, © Lotte Kramer. Reprinted by permission of Rockingham Press and the author.

Philip Larkin: 'Like the Train's Beat' from *Collected Poems*, © Philip Larkin. Reprinted by permission of Faber and Faber.

Alun Lewis: 'On Embarkation' from *Collected Poems*, 1994, © Alun Lewis. Reprinted by permission of Seren.

Frances Lovell: 'Train Journey' from *Envoi 90*, © Frances Lovell. Reprinted by permission of the author.

Martin J. Lowery: 'Delays and Departures' from *Envoi 109*, © Martin J. Lowery. Reprinted by permission of Envoi and the author.

Norman MacCaig: 'Sleeping Compartment' from *Old Maps and New: Selected Poems*, 1978, © Norman MacCaig. Reprinted by permission of Hogarth Press.

Roger McGough: 'Waving at Trains' from *Blazing Fruit*, 1989, © Roger McGough. Reprinted by permission of Penguin.

Louis MacNeice: 'Slow Movement' and 'Corner Seat' from *Selected Poems*, 1964, © Louis MacNeice. Reprinted by permission of Faber and Faber.

Mary Mestecky: 'First Train to Devil's Bridge', © Mary Mestecky. Reprinted by permission of the author.

Edna St Vincent Millay: 'Travel', from *Selected Poems. The Centenary Edition*, © Edna St Vincent Millay. Reprinted by permission of Carcanet and Elizabeth Barnett.

John Mole: 'The Home Front' from *Poetry Review*, vol. 83, no. 4, 1994, © John Mole. Reprinted by permission of the author.

Mollie Moorhill: 'Old Woman on a Train' from *A Few Late Leaves*, 1978, © Mollie Moorhill. Reprinted by permission of Yew Tree Books and Richard Rallings.

Edwin Morgan: 'Aberdeen Train' from *Penguin Modern Poets*, 1969, © Edwin Morgan. Reprinted by permission of Carcanet.

Jenny Morris: 'To Frances Cornford' from *Urban Space*, 1991, © Jenny Morris. Reprinted by permission of the National Poetry Foundation and the author.

Vincent Morrison: 'The Schonau Express' from *The Season of Comfort*, 1979, © Vincent Morrison. Reprinted by permission of Bloodaxe Books.

Graham Mort: 'To Lethe on the 8.10' from *Poetry Review*, vol. 83, no. 4,

1993, © Graham Mort. Reprinted by permission of the author.

Edwin Muir: 'The Wayside Station', © Edwin Muir.

Robin Munro: 'The Galloway Line' from *Poetry Review 68*, © Robin Munro.

P. Alamie Page: 'A Placid Gentleman' from *Envoi 22*, © P. Alamie Page. Reprinted by permission of Envoi.

David Palmer: 'Branch Line' from *Poetry Review*, vol. 67, no. 4, 1978, © David Palmer. Reprinted by permission of the author.

M.R. Peacocke: 'By the Way' from *Poetry Review*, vol. 77, no. 4, 1988 and 'Railway Allotments' from *Marginal Land*, 1988, reprinted by permission of Peterloo Poets, © M.R. Peacocke. Reprinted by permission of the author.

Patricia Pogson: 'Daniel' from *Staple 24* and 'Sleeper' from *The New Lake Poets*, © Patricia Pogson. Reprinted by permission of Bloodaxe Books and the author.

Peggy Poole: 'One Way Journey' from *Cherry Stones and Other Poems*, reprinted by permission of Headland Publications, 'Taking her Work Home' from *Iota*, 'Intercity' from *Envoi 90*, reprinted by permission of Envoi and 'Unchecked', © Peggy Poole.

Roy Powell: 'Exchange Station' from *Poetry Merseyside*, 1981, © Roy Powell.

Andrew Pye: 'Privacy' from *Staple 30*, 1994, © Andrew Pye. Reprinted by permission of Staple and the author.

Bartholomew Quinn: 'Signalman' from *Poetry Introduction 1*, © Bartholomew Quinn. Reprinted by permission of Faber and Faber and the author.

Mike Rathbone: 'No Day Returns' from *Making Waves*, © Mike Rathbone. Reprinted by permission of the author.

Mike Read: 'Effingham Station' from *Poet's England: Surrey*, © Mike Read. Reprinted by permission of Brentham Press and the author.

Frank Rickards: 'Girl in a Train' from *Girl in a Train*, © Frank Rickards. Reprinted by permission of the author.

Rod Riesco: 'Announcement' from *Orbis 95*, © Rod Riesco. Reprinted by permission of the author.

Frances Sackett: 'Travel Notes', © Frances Sackett. Reprinted by permission of the author.

Lawrence Sail: 'Departures' from *Out of Hand*, 1992, © Lawrence Sail. Reprinted by permission of Bloodaxe Books and the author.

Peter Sansom: 'Transpennine', © Peter Sansom. Reprinted by permission of Carcanet and the author.

Siegfried Sassoon: 'Morning Express', © George Sassoon. Reprinted by permission of George Sassoon.

Susan Saunders: 'Excursion' from *Acumen 20*, © Susan Saunders. Reprinted by permission of Acumen and the author.

William Scammell: 'Trains' from *PN Review* and *Bleeding Heart Yard*, © William Scammell. Reprinted by permission of Peterloo Poets and the author.

Amy Jo Schoonover: 'Train Whistles' from *New and Used Poems*, © Amy Jo Schoonover. Reprinted by permission of the author.

Meg Seaton: 'Ghost Train' from *New Poetry*, no. 49, 1980, © Meg Seaton. Reprinted by permission of Peterloo Poets.

Howard Sergeant: 'Making the Connection' and 'The End of the Line' from *A Fairground Familiar*, © Jean Sergeant. Reprinted by permission of Rivelin Press, Headland Publications and Jean Sergeant.

Jean Sergeant: 'Suspense at Preston', © Jean Sergeant. Reprinted by permission of the author.

Carol Shergold: 'Vanishing Point', © Carol Shergold. Reprinted by permission of Peterloo Poets and the author.

Susan Skinner: 'No Return' from *Acumen 23*, © Susan Skinner. Reprinted by permission by Acumen and the author.

Iain Crichton Smith: 'The Journey' from *New Poetry 48*, 1980, © Iain Crichton Smith. Reprinted by permission of Carcanet.

Stephen Spender: 'The Express' from *Collected Poems*, 1928–1985, © Stephen Spender. Reprinted by permission of Faber and Faber.

Pauline Stainer: 'Between Stations' from *The Ice-Pilot Speaks*, 1994, © Pauline Stainer. Reprinted by permission of Bloodaxe Books and the author.

Michael Standen: 'Fellow-Travelling' from *Poetry Review 67*, © Michael Standen. Reprinted by permission of Flambard Press and the author.

Kenneth Steven: 'Remembering Peter' and 'The Train' from *Remembering Peter*. © Kenneth Steven. Reprinted by permission of the National Poetry Foundation and the author.

Mandy Sutter: 'Trains' from *Envoi 104*, © Mandy Sutter. Reprinted by permission of Envoi and the author.

David Sutton: 'From the Train' from *Poetry Review*, vol. 80, no. 3, 1990, © David Sutton. Reprinted by permission of the author.

Malcolm Taylor: 'Breakfast Call', © Malcolm Taylor. Reprinted by permission of BBC North and the author.

John Tickner: 'Hobo Sapiens', © John Tickner. Reprinted by permission of the author.

Hilary Tinsley: 'Tank Engines Rule – O.K?', © Hilary Tinsley. Reprinted by permission of the author.

Margaret Toms: 'Grand Central Railway' from *Clay's Bright Soul*, 1992, ©
Margaret Toms. Reprinted by permission of the National Poetry Foundation
and the author.

Dennis Travis: 'Broadening the Mind', © Dennis Travis. Reprinted by permission of BBC North and the author.

Sylvia Turner: 'Hold-up' from *Staple 26*, © Sylvia Turner. Reprinted by
permission of Staple and the author.

Peter Walton: 'Ghost Train' and 'Impatience' from *Out of Season*, 1977,
'Natural Break' from *Poetry Review*, vol. 69, © Peter Walton. Reprinted by
permission of the author.

John Ward: 'Engines in the National Railway Museum, York' from *A Late
Harvest*, 1982, reprinted by permission of Peterloo Poets, 'Liverpool Overhead Railway in the Thirties' from *Both Sides of the River*, reprinted by
permission of Headland Publications, 'Labourers on the Settle–Carlisle Railway' from *Grandfather Best and the Protestant Work Ethic*, 1991, reprinted
by permission of Littlewood Arc, 'Somewhere North of Wolverhampton'
from *A Kind of Likeness*, 1985, reprinted by permission of Littlewood Press
and 'Terminus' from *A Late Harvest*, 1982, © John Ward, reprinted by
permission of Peterloo Poets and the author.

Dick Wilkinson: 'Was it You at Warrington?' from *Poetry Review 71*, © Dick
Wilkinson. Reprinted by permission of the author.

Mary Wilson: 'Reply to the Laureate' from *Selected Poems*, 1970, © Mary
Wilson. Reprinted by permission of Hutchinson and the author.

Jonathan Wood: 'The Guard's Van', © Jonathan Wood. Reprinted by permission of BBC North and the author.

Marguerite Wood: 'Past the City Cemetery' from *A Wall Cracks*, © Marguerite Wood. Reprinted by permission by the National Poetry Foundation
and the author.

Chris Woods: 'The Space Age of the Train', © Chris Woods. Reprinted by
permission of Enitharmon Press and the author.

Judith Young: 'Returning Home' from *The Glen and Other Places*, © Judith
Young. Reprinted by permission of the author.

Anon: 'The Spiritual Railway'. Reproduced by permission of the Dean and
Chapter, Ely Cathedral.

INDEX OF FIRST LINES

INDEX OF POETS